Matthew Lopez

THE INHERITANCE

Matthew Lopez is the author of *The Whipping Man* (Luna Stage Company, Manhattan Theatre Club), *The Legend of Georgia McBride* (Denver Center for the Performing Arts, Manhattan Class Company, Geffen Playhouse), *Somewhere* (The Old Globe, Hartford Stage Company), *Reverberation* (Hartford Stage Company) and *Zoey's Perfect Wedding* (Denver Center for the Performing Arts). In London, he was represented in Headlong Theatre's 9/11 Decade anthology with his play *The Sentinels*.

MATTHEW LOPEZ

The Inheritance

inspired by the novel Howards End *by*
E. M. FORSTER

FABER & FABER

First published in 2018
by Faber and Faber Ltd
The Bindery, 51 Hatton Garden
London EC1N 8HN

New edition with revised text, 2018

This third edition with revised text, 2020

Typeset by Country Setting, Kingsdown, Kent CT14 8ES
Printed in England by CPI Group (UK) Ltd, Croydon CR0 4YY

A CIP record for this book is available from the British Library

978-0-571-36226-4

MIX
Paper | Supporting
responsible forestry
FSC
www.fsc.org   FSC® C171272

Printed and bound in the UK on FSC® certified paper in line with our continuing
commitment to ethical business practices, sustainability and the environment.
For further information see faber.co.uk/environmental-policy

For Brandon

The Inheritance was originally commissioned by Hartford Stage (Darko Tresnjak, Artistic Director; Michael Stotts, Managing Director). The world premiere was performed in London at the Young Vic, Part One on 2 March 2018, and Part Two on 9 March 2018. The cast, in alphabetical order, was as follows:

Young Man 7 / Jasper Hugo Bolton
Young Man 5 / Charles / Peter / Agent Robert Boulter
Young Man 10 / Toby Darling Andrew Burnap
Young Man 3 / Young Henry / Tucker Hubert Burton
Henry Wilcox John Benjamin Hickey
Morgan / Walter Paul Hilton
Young Man 1 / Adam / Leo Samuel H. Levine
Boy Sam Lockhart, Joshua De La Warr
Young Man 6 / Tristan Syrus Lowe
Young Man 2 / Jason 1 / Paul / Doorman Michael Marcus
Margaret Vanessa Redgrave
Young Man 9 / Eric Glass Kyle Soller
Young Man 4 / Young Walter / Clinic Worker Luke Thallon
Young Man 8 / Jason 2 / Other Agent Michael Walters

Direction Stephen Daldry
Design Bob Crowley
Light Jon Clark
Sound Paul Arditti and Christopher Reid
Music Paul Englishby
UK Casting Julia Horan CDG
US Casting Jordan Thaler CSA and Heidi Griffiths CSA
Associate Director Justin Martin
Dramaturg Elizabeth Williamson
Dialect William Conacher
Fights Terry King
Assistant Director Sadie Spencer

Executive Producer David Lan

This production was supported by Nattering Way LLC and Sonia Friedman Productions.

Andrew Burnap, John Benjamin Hickey and Samuel H. Levine appeared with the permission of UK Equity, incorporating the Variety Artistes' Federation, pursuant to an exchange programme between American Equity and UK Equity.

Sadie Spencer was supported by the Jerwood Assistant Directors Programme at the Young Vic.

The Inheritance transferred to the Noël Coward Theatre in the West End of London, with a first performance of Part One on 21 September 2018 and of Part Two on 28 September 2018. The cast, in alphabetical order, was as follows:

Young Man 7 / Jasper Hugo Bolton
Young Man 5 / Charles / Peter / Agent Robert Boulter
Young Man 10 / Toby Darling Andrew Burnap
Young Man 3 / Young Henry / Tucker Hubert Burton
Henry Wilcox John Benjamin Hickey
Morgan / Walter Paul Hilton
Young Man 1 / Adam / Leo Samuel H. Levine
Young Man 6 / Tristan Syrus Lowe
Boy Harrison March-Ward, Anthony Zac Moran, Joshua De La Warr
Young Man 2 / Jason 1 / Paul / Doorman Michael Marcus
Margaret Vanessa Redgrave
Young Man 4 / Young Walter / Clinic Worker Jack Riddiford
Young Man 9 / Eric Glass Kyle Soller
Young Man 8 / Jason 2 / Other Agent Michael Walters

Direction Stephen Daldry
Design Bob Crowley
Light Jon Clark
Sound Paul Arditti and Christopher Reid
Music Paul Englishby
UK Casting Julia Horan CDG
US Casting Jordan Thaler CSA and Heidi Griffiths CSA
Executive Producer David Lan
Associate Director Justin Martin
Dramaturg Elizabeth Williamson
Dialect William Conacher
Fights Terry King
Resident Director Jane Moriarty

The Young Vic production was presented in the West
End by Tom Kirdahy, Sonia Friedman Productions and
Hunter Arnold with Elizabeth Dewberry & Ali Ahmet
Kocabiyik, 1001 Nights Productions, Greg Berlanti,
Brad Blume, Shane Ewen, Rupert Gavin, Robert Greenblatt,
Marguerite Hoffman, Mark Lee, Peter May, Arnon
Milchan, Oliver Roth, Scott Rudin, Tulchin/Bartner
Productions, Bruno Wang, Richard Winkler, Bruce
Cohen/Scott M. Delman.

The Inheritance in this revised version opened at the Ethel Barrymore Theatre, New York, with a first performance on 17 November 2019. The cast, in alphabetical order, was as follows:

Young Man 6 / Tristan Jordan Barbour

Boy Ryan M. Buggle, Tre Ryder

Young Man 5 / Toby's Agent / Charles Wilcox
   Jonathan Burke

Toby Darling Andrew Burnap

Young Man 2 / Jason 1 / Toby's Doorman / Agent
   Darryl Gene Daughtry Jr.

Young Man 4 / Young Walter / Tucker Dylan Frederick

Young Man 7 / Jasper / Paul Wilcox Kyle Harris

Henry Wilcox John Benjamin Hickey

Morgan / Walter Poole Paul Hilton

Adam / Leo Samuel H. Levine

Young Man 3 / Young Henry Carson Mccalley

Margaret Lois Smith

Eric Glass Kyle Soller

Young Man 8 / Jason 2 / Clinic Worker
   Arturo Luis Soria

Designed by Bob Crowley
Directed by Stephen Daldry
Lighting Design Jon Clark
Sound Design Paularditti and Christopher Reid
Original Music Paul Englishby
Associate Director Justin Martin
Casting Jordan Thaler CSA, Heidi Griffiths CSA,
  Julia Horan CDG
Dramaturg Elizabeth Williamson
Advertising / Marketing AKA
Press Representative Polk and Co
Social Media Marathon Digital
Technical Supervision Hudson Theatrical Associates
Production Stage Manager Jill Cordle
Company Manager Steve Lukens
UK General Management Sonia Friedman Productions
US General Management RCI Theatricals

The New York production was presented on Broadway
by Tom Kirdahy, Sonia Friedman Productions, Hunter
Arnold, Elizabeth Dewberry & Ali Ahmet Kocabiyik,
1001 Nights Productions, Robert Greenblatt, Mark Lee,
Peter May, Scott Rudin, Richard Winkler, Bruce Cohen,
Mara Isaacs, Greg Berlanti & Robbie Rogers, Brad
Blume, Burnt Umber Productions, Shane Ewen, Greenleaf
Productions, Marguerite Hoffman, Oliver Roth, Joseph
Baker/Drew Hodges, Stephanie P. McClelland, Broadway
Strategic Return Fund, Caiola Productions, Mary J.
Davis, Kayla Greenspan, Fakston Productions, FBK
Productions, Sally Cade Holmes, Benjamin Lowy, MWM

Live, Lee & Alec Seymour, Lorenzo Thione, Sing Out, Louise! Productions, AB Company/Julie Boardman, Adam Zell & Co/ZKM Media, Jamie Deroy/Catherine Adler, Desantis-Baugh Productions/Adam Hyndman, Gary Dimauro/Meredith Lynsey Schade, John Goldwyn/Silva Theatrical Group, Deborah Green/Christina Mattsson, Cliff Hopkins/George Scarles, Invisible Wall Productions/Lauren Stein, Sharon Karmazin/Broadway Factor NYC, Brian Spector/Madeleine Foster Bersin, Undivided Productions/Hysell Dohr Group, Ushkowitzlatimer Productions/Tyler Mount.

Characters

E. M. Forster ('Morgan')
Eric Glass
Toby Darling
Walter Poole
Adam McDowell
Henry Wilcox
Leo
Margaret

Young Man 1
Young Man 2
Young Man 3
Young Man 4
Young Man 5
Young Man 6
Young Man 7
Young Man 8
Young Man 9
Young Man 10
Tristan
Jasper
Jason 1
Jason 2
Charles Wilcox
Paul Wilcox
Tucker
Toby's Agent
Dealer
Clinic Worker
Doorman 1
Doorman 2
Assistant
Toby's Other Agent

THE INHERITANCE

Hidden

From all I did and from all I said
they shouldn't try to find out who I was.
An obstacle was there and it distorted
my actions and the way I lived my life.
An obstacle was there and it stopped me
on many occasions when I was going to speak.
The most unnoticed of my actions
and the most covert of all my writings:
from these alone will they come to know me.
But perhaps it's not worth squandering
so much care and trouble on puzzling me out.
Afterwards – in some more perfect society –
someone else who's fashioned like me
will surely appear and be free to do as he pleases.

Constantine Cavafy (1908)
translated by Daniel Mendelsohn

Part One

Prologue

A handful of Young Men sitting around writing. Some with notebooks, some on laptops. Off to the side, apart from the group, one lone young man sits. We shall call him Young Man 1.

Young Man 1 He has a story to tell – it is banging around inside him, aching to come out. But how does he begin? He opens his favorite novel, hoping to find inspiration in its first familiar sentence. And in reading those words, he finds himself once again in the gentle, reassuring presence of their author.

An older man enters. He is E. M. Forster. We, like all his intimates, shall call him Morgan.

Morgan I hope I'm not disturbing you.

Young Man 2 No, please!

Young Man 6 Join us!

Young Man 5 You're not disturbing us at all.

Young Man 7 We could use the distraction.

Morgan How's the work coming?

They groan in frustration.

Young Man 2 It's going terribly.

Young Man 3 I hate everything I've written today.

Young Man 4 I'm a total fraud.

Young Man 5 Others have said this better than I ever will.

Young Man 6 I have nothing original to say.

Young Man 7 All my work is derivative.

Young Man 8 My characters won't do what I want them to.

Young Man 9 I've been writing this same sentence for seven hours.

Young Man 10 I think I'm a fucking genius.

Morgan (*to Young Man 1*) Why aren't you writing?

Young Man 1 I don't know how to start. I thought that maybe I'd read a little and see how others begin their stories.

Morgan You have stumbled across the writer's most valuable tool: procrastination.
    What is your story about?

Young Man 1 Me. My friends. The men I've loved. And those I've lost.

Morgan Goodness me. Friendship, love, loss. Sounds like you're off to a very good start.

Young Man 1 But the thing is I'm not! My ideas refuse to become words.

Morgan Yes, I understand. All your ideas are at the starting post, ready to run. And yet they all must pass through a keyhole in order to begin the race.

Young Man 1 I picked up one of your novels –

Morgan Which one? Ah, *Howards End*.

Young Man 1 'One may as well begin with Helen's letters to her sister.' God, what a great first sentence! So dashed off, as if to suggest it doesn't really matter how you start.

Morgan Perhaps it doesn't.

Young Man 1 I keep returning to this book again and again.

Morgan Tell me: what is it about my novel that speaks to you? What do you find in its pages?

Young Man 2 Guidance?

Young Man 8 Compassion.

Young Man 4 Wisdom.

Young Man 5 I love its humanity.

Young Man 7 Its honesty.

Young Man 1 It comforts me.

Young Man 10 Not me. I mean, it's a great book, don't get me wrong. And the movie's . . . also good. But, I mean, the world is so different now. I can't identify with it at all.

Young Man 9 It's a hundred years old.

Young Man 7 The world has changed so much.

Young Man 3 Our lives are nothing like the people in your book.

Morgan How can that be true? Hearts still love, don't they? And break. Hope, fear, jealousy, desire. Your lives may be different. But surely the feelings are the same. The difference is merely setting, context, costumes. But those are just details.

Young Man 1 I have plenty of details. What I don't have is a beginning.

Morgan Why do you need to tell your story?

Young Man 1 To understand it. To understand myself.

Morgan That's a story I'd like to hear.

Young Man 1 Will you help me tell my story? Our story?

Young Man 7 Who we are.

Young Man 6 How we got here.

Young Man 4 And what we mean to each other.

Morgan I would be delighted.
      So, to begin: who does your story start with?

Young Man 1 Toby.

Morgan One may as well begin with Toby's . . . what?

Young Man 1 Voicemails.

Morgan One may as well begin with Toby's voicemails –

Young Man 1 – to his boyfriend.

Act One

SCENE ONE

1. A Party at the Hamptons

Young Man 10 becomes Toby Darling.

Young Man 1 BEEP!

Toby You are going to *die* when I tell you what you're missing. Call me back.

Young Man 1 Toby's had a martini. *Beep!*

Toby Where are you? You can't be asleep already. You are missing the most exquisite party, holy shit! Call me when you get this. God, I love the Hamptons!

Young Man 1 Toby's had another martini. *Beep!*

Toby Okay. So. First of all, this house is *gorgeous*. It's this sleek, modernist saltbox, all concrete and glass with a massive infinity pool that stretches out to the ocean. And all of it so tastefully decorated, you would *die*.

Young Man 1 And its owner, Henry Wilcox?

Toby Oh, Henry Wilcox! You were right: Henry Wilcox is really kinda dreamy. I want to be him when I grow up. He's wearing the most magnificent suit, which was made by this Saville Row-trained tailor on the Upper West Side. And when I asked him for the guy's information, Henry says:

Young Man 1 'Oh Toby, he's way out of your price range.'

Toby Which is such a dick thing to say and yet coming from the mouth of Henry Wilcox, I was simply dazzled.

Oh! And we played football today. Tackle, not touch. Can you imagine me playing football?

Lads No!

Toby Well, I didn't. But I could have if I wanted and that's the point.

Young Man 1 And Henry's partner – Walter Poole?

Toby Oh, Walter! How do I describe Walter? Walter has this sort of, I don't know, this ghost-like spirit about him. Like a sheer curtain in front of an open window. He's like Valium. I love him.

Then:

Holy shit, Meryl Streep is here! Eric, this party is *ridiculous*. Call me back!

Young Man 1 Toby's had five martinis. *Beep!*

Toby Walter just said I could stay the whole weekend! Pack a bag, bring me some underwear, and get your ass on a train first thing tomorrow morning. You are going to love it here!

Young Man 1 New York City is a Darwinian experiment writ large. Every summer, waves of college graduates wash up on its shores to begin the struggle toward success and achievement.

Young Man 5 They are young, ambitious, intelligent and driven.

Young Man 8 Also helps if they're attractive.

Young Man 6 Each convinced they have the talents and abilities not just to survive in the city –

Young Man 2 – but also to thrive.

Young Man 1 Toby Darling and his boyfriend . . . Eric Glass, were two such strivers.

Young Man 9 becomes Eric Glass.

Morgan Let's have a look at them.
Right. So . . . neither were all that young anymore –

Toby Hey!

Morgan – nor particularly brilliant –

Eric Wait a second.

Morgan – or successful.

Toby Oh come on!

Morgan They didn't have two nickels to rub together. And yet, through no enterprise of their own, they were the inhabitants of an enormous three-bedroom, two-bathroom apartment with a terrace that overlooked the park on the fifteenth floor of an elegant pre-war building on the Upper West Side of Manhattan.
Eric Glass was packing a bag just as Toby walked into the apartment –

Young Man 1 – hungover and miserable.

2. *Eric and Toby's Apartment*

Eric Toby? I was just about to head to Penn Station.

Toby Didn't you get my voicemail?

Eric You left two dozen.

Toby The one from early this morning.

Eric No, I guess I / didn't –

Young Man 1 *Beep!*

Young Man 2 Hey, it's me.

Young Man 3 It's early.

Young Man 4 Like, maybe six?

Young Man 5 Look, change of plans.

Young Man 6 I'm taking the first train back.

Young Man 7 And please delete all my messages from last night.

Young Man 8 I wish I'd never come.

Eric What happened?

Toby I am so humiliated. I can never show my face there again. I can never leave this *apartment* again.

Eric Just tell me, babe.

Toby I threw up.

Eric Oh. That's not so bad. On the train?

Toby At the party.

Eric Oh. Well . . . like . . . on the lawn / or –?

Toby On their sofa.

Eric Oh.

Toby And their dog. Which was sitting in Meryl Streep's lap.
    I am beyond mortified. Alec Baldwin and Mariska Hargitay watched me projectile vomit over *the most transcendent and celebrated actor of all time!*

Eric It's not like it was Glenda Jackson or anything.

Toby You've seen *Sophie's Choice*! I am so humiliated.

Eric Oh, Toby. So what happened then?

Toby Meryl Streep just sat there, covered in vomit. The dog, it . . . oh God, the dog . . .

Eric Just tell me –

Toby It started licking it off her face.
Are you laughing?

Eric Not *at* you.

Toby Thank *God* for Walter, who acted as if this sort of thing happens all the time in East Hampton. He helped the world's most beloved actor out of the room. Then he brought me a ginger ale and helped me up to my room. I woke up around five and Ubered over to the train station before the sun came up.

Eric You left without saying goodbye?

Toby Well, I wasn't going to stick around for breakfast!

Eric Oh, Toby . . .

Eric takes out his phone.

Toby What are you doing?

Eric I'm calling Walter.

Toby No, please!

Eric We can't just say nothing.

Toby Yes we can! I promise they'll forget all about us by next week.

Eric I don't want them to forget about us. I like Henry and Walter.

Toby Please just let it be!

Eric reluctantly puts his phone away.

God, I'm such a mess.

Eric You've puked all over this city and lived to show your face again.

Toby Yes, but never in the Hamptons. Everyone at that party was so cool and unaffected, like they belonged there.

Eric They *did* belong there. Maybe someday we'll have money and we'll belong there, too. Or maybe that's just not us and we'll belong somewhere else.

Toby It *has* to be us. You didn't see that house, Eric.

Then, truly bummed:

Aw. You didn't see that house. I'm sorry I ruined our beach vacation.

Eric It was a plan for all of a minute. I barely had time to cancel anything. In fact, I was planning to noodle around the Whitney today. Maybe go to Film Forum. You wanna come?

Toby I'm so hungover, babe. I just wanna fall asleep and wake up in my forties.

Eric Oh, Toby.
   Go to sleep. I'll be home to make you dinner.

Toby Call me before you head to the movies. I might just rally.

Morgan What does Eric do now?

Young Man 1 I think he calls Walter anyway.

Morgan And who is Walter?

Young Man 1 You are.

Morgan becomes Walter Poole.

Walter Hello?

Eric Hi, Walter? It's Eric Glass.

Walter Well hello, Eric Glass. I wondered if I might hear from you today.

Eric Yeah. So listen, about last night, Toby feels just awful.

Walter Judging from the number of martinis Toby had, I'm not surprised.

Eric Listen, are you sure there isn't there something we can do? I can send a check / or maybe call a –

Walter What you can do is to put it out of your mind.

Eric Well . . . I'll try.

Walter Now if you'll excuse me, the steam cleaners have just arrived. Totally unrelated to the events of last night I assure you. So nice to hear from you, Eric.

Walter hangs up, becomes Morgan again.

Morgan Eric Glass loved people. He would open his home regularly to his old friends and new acquaintances.

Young Man 1 He cooked elaborate dinners for all the fascinating people he collected over the years, listening to their stories –

Morgan – rarely offering his own in return.

Young Man 1 When someone new entered his orbit, he instantly made them feel part of the family.

Morgan He shared his passions, shared his books – even when he knew they wouldn't be returned.

Young Man 1 And so it was, on Friday, October 9, 2015 that Eric Glass opened his home to his friends to celebrate his thirty-third birthday. He served dinner, poured wine, and played for them a piece of music that had recently captured his ear.

End of Scene One.

October 9, 2015. Eric's Thirty-Third Birthday

1. Eric and Toby's Apartment

Eric and Toby with a group of four other young men. Ravel's String Quartet in F Major plays.

Eric Toby and I heard a group from Juilliard playing this piece today at the Strand.

Tristan Who's it by?

Eric Ravel.

Jason 2 I don't really know Ravel. What's he done?

Jason 1 What do you mean, 'done', babe?

Eric 'Bolero'.

Jason 2 Which one's that?

Eric has to start dah-dah-dahing 'Bolero'.

Jason 2 Oh right! Torvill and Dean. And he wrote this?

Eric Yes.

Tristan It's so captivating.

Eric Isn't it?

Jason 2 I think I once heard this in a movie.

Jasper Yeah, me too. *Atonement*, maybe?

Jason 2 Or *English Patient*? Something English.

Jason 1 It sounds like the Ewok music from *Return of the Jedi*.

Jason 2 *Aye que* cute those little Ewoks!

Eric Here, let me skip to the second movement.

He skips ahead in the piece.

Isn't that nice? I love all that plucking.

Toby Eric's into hard-core plucking.

Tristan It sounds like the bubbles in a glass of champagne.

Eric Yeah, I hear that.

Jason 2 Or a bumblebee racing around a meadow.

Eric Yeah, I hear that too. All right, I'm gonna check on dinner.

Young Man 1 Excuse me.

Eric Hey babe, can you open another bottle of wine?

Toby Absolutely.

Young Man 1 Excuse me?

Tristan What are you making? It smells so good.

Eric I decided to splurge for my birthday and I got this beautiful leg of lamb at Dickson's.

Young Man 1 enters, carrying a bag from the Strand.

Young Man 1 Excuse me. I'm so sorry to interrupt your party. Do you remember me?

Eric No.

Young Man 1 I was sitting next to you today at the Strand. Do you remember me?

Eric Sorry . . .

Young Man 1 When they were playing that music? (*To Toby.*) Do you remember me?

Toby Oh yeah, the twink who asked us what piece they were playing.

Young Man 1 Yes.

Jason 2 It's Ravel.

Eric And now you're here.

Young Man 1 Yes.

Toby Why are you here?

Young Man 1 It's my bag.

Toby The bag in your hands?

Young Man 1 No, that bag over there.

He points to another Strand bag on the floor.

Young Man 1 I think you took my bag.

Toby What?

Young Man 1 Accidentally. We both had our bags on the floor and when you left, I think you may have grabbed mine. Accidentally.

Eric Oh my God, we are so sorry. Toby, you did again!

Jason 1 'Again'? You mean he's done this before?

Eric Constantly! He's always taking things that don't belong to him. Scarves, gloves, umbrellas.

Jasper Virginity.

Eric Seriously baby, you're becoming a real kleptomaniac.

Toby I didn't even notice.

Eric We are so sorry about that.

Young Man 1 You're Toby Darling, right? (*To Eric.*) He wrote the book *Loved Boy*?

Jasper } Oh wow, that just happened.
Tristan } Toby, you just got recognized.

Jason 1 ⎫ That's pretty cool.
Jason 2 ⎭ You're famous!

Toby Is that why you're here? You read my book, it changed your life, you saw me in the bookstore and so you followed me home for an autograph, making up a story about switched bags?

Young Man 1 Actually, you left your wallet in the bag.

The Lads die laughing at this.

Also . . .

He removes six copies of the same book from the bag.

Jason 1 Is that your book, Toby?

Jasper You bought six copies of your own book?

Tristan Oh Toby, you crack me up.

Toby Yeah, laugh it up, guys. If you must know, I promised the ladies on the ninth floor that I would bring them each a signed copy for their book club.

Eric Have you read Toby's book?

Young Man 1 No, but I –

Jason 2 So what books did *you* get?

Jason 2 grabs Young Man 1's bag.

Young Man 1 Oh, I'm –

Jason 2 A Cavafy collection.

Eric Ooh, which translation?

Jason 1 Mendelsohn.

Eric ⎫ The best.
Jason 1 ⎭ I've been meaning to get that.

Jason 2 *Giovanni's Room. Call Me By Your Name. The*

Swimming-Pool Library.

Jason 1 I'm sensing a theme here.

Toby You're buying all these queer books, why didn't you buy mine?

Tristan Because you'd already bought every copy in the store, Toby.

Jason 2 You should turn it into a movie, Toby.

Jason 1 Yes! It would make a great movie!

Toby Actually – (*To Eric.*) Should I tell them?

Eric It's your news, babe.

Toby Yeah, but nothing's official yet.

Jason 1 Oh wow, he *is* turning it into a movie!

Toby No, *but* – I have been commissioned to turn it into a play.

Silence. Then –

Jason 2 A musical?

Toby No, a straight play.

Eric Well . . .

Jason 2 Will there be any music in it?

Toby I don't know, I haven't written it yet.

Jason 1 I could totally see it as a play, Toby.

Toby Thank you.

Tristan Toby, that's amazing. / Congratulations.

Jasper Yeah Toby, good for you.

Toby Thank you. I'm really excited.

Eric It's going to be an amazing play.

Jason 2 Just be sure to put some music in it.

Toby (*to Young Man 1*) Do you want to take a copy?

Young Man 1 You don't have to / give me –

Toby Would you read it or would you just throw it on a shelf?

Young Man 1 No, I'd read it.

Toby Then it's your book.

Young Man 1 Thank you. I should let you get back to your / party.

    The Lads protest.

Eric ⎫ No, stay.
Jason 2 ⎭ It's Eric's birthday!

Young Man 1 Happy birthday.

Eric Thank you. Are you hungry? I made tons of food.

Young Man 1 Oh, I couldn't –

Tristan Eric is an amazing cook.

Eric Or maybe a glass of wine? We were just listening to the piece they were playing at the Strand.

Young Man 1 Oh God, I really loved that piece.

Eric Yeah, me too. It's beautiful, isn't it?

Young Man 1 Yeah. It . . . it yearns.

Eric Yes, it does! That is the perfect word. I think it's about mourning.

Young Man 1 Oh interesting.

Eric You don't agree?

Young Man 1 I think . . . I think maybe it's about unrequited love.

Eric Really? How?

Young Man 1 It's romantic but in a way that feels unresolved.

Jason 2 Funny, I don't hear that at all.

Young Man 1 Maybe I'm wrong.

Eric Don't let them bully you.

Young Man 1 Okay. Well, in the first movement, the phrases are legato, rising and falling, like breath – no – like a sigh. I imagine someone looking at photos of someone they've loved for a long time. Then the second movement starts with plucking instead of bowing. It's summery and fresh. It makes me think of a butterfly flitting through a meadow.

Jason 2 I said a bumblebee.

Young Man 1 But then halfway through the second movement, the sadness returns, as if our character suddenly sees the object of their desire in the flesh. That painful, yearning feeling when you want someone so badly but can never have them. Then the last movement is like a raging fire that completely consumes the person. Burned alive by their own desire.

Toby A raging fire? You got all that from listening to it once at a bookstore?

Young Man 1 That's just the way my brain works.

Eric You're not drinking your wine.

Young Man 1 Oh, I don't / really –

Eric Do you want something else?

Toby Maybe something stronger?

Young Man 1 Oh, no / I –

Eric I could make you a cocktail.

Toby Eric makes a mean Manhattan.

Jason 2 Ooh, I want a Manhattan!

Tristan Yeah, me too.

Toby Eric, you have been commissioned to make Manhattans.

Eric Yes! On it!

Tristan You're gonna be crawling home, I promise.

Toby So what's your story, kid?

Jason 1 Are you in school?

Jason 2 How old are you?

Tristan Where are you from?

Jasper Do you have a boyfriend?

All eyes on Young Man 1.

Young Man 1 I should probably go.

A great protest from the Lads.

Eric Oh no, stay. Please.
We've got tons of food, lots of good wine.

Young Man 1 No, I should go. Thank you, though.

Eric Will you come back, then? Now that you know where we live?

Young Man 1 Thank you. I . . . thanks.

Young Man 1 grabs his bag, exits. Eric looks at his friends.

Eric You are all just the worst.

Tristan ⎱ Don't look at me.
Jasper ⎰ We just asked him about himself.

Eric You couldn't have made him feel just a little more welcome? Did you hear how he talked about that piece of music? And we chased him away.

Toby So look him up on Facebook.

Eric Yes! Good idea, Toby. What was his name?

They all stare at each other blankly.

Toby Who wants a Manhattan?

2. *Eric Interlude*

Morgan Eric Glass did not keep many secrets. But there was one truth he kept to himself, even from Toby.

Eric What truth is that?

Morgan Eric Glass did not believe he was special. He was not as brilliant or as accomplished as his friends. He thought of himself – in all things and in all ways – as painfully ordinary. Whilst admiring the fearlessness in others, he was, in his own life, cautious.

Eric Eric had taken the first job he was offered out of college, working for his friend Jasper, whose brilliance he glimpsed from their earliest days as classmates as Yale.

Jasper Jasper started his own company at the age of twenty-one, working as a social justice entrepreneur. Eric was his first employee.

Eric He met Tristan his first year after college. They went on three dates –

Young Man 6 – and decided they were each other's best friend. Tristan is a physician.

Eric He works in the emergency room at NYU Medical Center.
Eric met Jason while working as volunteers on the Kerry campaign in 2004.

Young Man 8 We lost that election but the friendship remains. Jason is a first-grade teacher.

Young Man 2 Yes! And his boyfriend –

Young Man 8 No, his partner –

Young Man 2 His partner, whose name is / Stephen –

Young Man 8 – also named Jason –

Young Man 2 Right, his partner, also named Jason is a / human rights –

Young Man 8 – high school science teacher!

Young Man 2 Yes, okay fine. *But* – they're not just partners –

Young Man 2 pulls out two wedding bands from his pocket. Young Man 2 slips a ring onto Young Man 8's finger.

Young Man 2 They're married.

Morgan To each other?

Young Man 2 Yes, of course.

Young Man 8 I do I do I do I do I do!

Young Man 2 and Young Man 8 kiss.

Morgan Are all of you married?

Tristan Find me a man who is worth a damn and I will marry the son of a bitch.

Morgan What about Jasper?

Jasper Jasper is not the marrying kind.

Morgan Why not?

Young Man 6 Jasper dates young guys.

Young Man 4 Like, just-out-of-college young?

Jasper Jasper doesn't like complicated men.

Morgan Are Eric and Toby married?

Young Man 1 Not yet.

Young Man 3 I have a question:

Morgan Yes?

Young Man 3 How can Eric afford such a nice apartment?

Young Man 7 Yeah, I was wondering that too.

Morgan In order to understand who Eric Glass is, one first has to understand the significance of his family's apartment on the Upper West Side.

Young Man 1 Eric's grandfather, Nathan, was a veteran of the 10th Armored Division, which helped liberate Dachau. His grandmother, Miriam, a refugee from Germany.

Morgan In the fall of 1947, they signed the lease on a rent-controlled apartment on West End Avenue. This was back when middle-class families could afford such places.

Eric This apartment became the first place Eric's grandmother felt safe in the world. She raised her family here in this apartment. She voted in every election at the public school around the corner. She watched John Kennedy's death, Richard Nixon's resignation, and Barack Obama's election from the living room of this apartment. It was in this apartment that Miriam Glass became an American.

Young Man 1 After her death in December 2008, Eric took up residence in the apartment in order to continue the family's claim on the dwelling. He met Toby Darling a week later.

Toby Toby Darling entered Eric's life like a typhoon.

Morgan Eric recognized within the first few minutes of their first date Toby's potential for greatness.

Young Man 1 And also his capacity for destruction.

Eric Both possibilities attracted him.

Young Man 1 The two instantly fell in love and Toby moved in four months later.

Eric For Eric, it was everything he'd ever wanted in a relationship.

Toby For Toby, it was . . .

Morgan For Toby, it was a home that was safe and stable and loving.

Young Man 1 Toby inspired Eric. Eric protected Toby.

Toby Toby fucked the living daylights out of Eric.

Eric Eric and Toby had really great sex.

Morgan Thank you, gentlemen. Now that we know what Eric cares about most, we must give him something to fight against. A few days before Christmas that year, Eric receives a call from his father informing him that the building's management company has finally decided to begin eviction proceedings against the Glass family.

Eric No, please not that.

Young Man 1 They're hiring a lawyer and planning to fight it.

Morgan But it is possible that 2016 could be Eric's last year living in his family's cherished home.
  What would Eric do after receiving such news?

Eric He would want to be comforted by Toby.

Morgan Is Toby particularly good at providing comfort?

Eric Well . . .

Young Man 1 No.

Morgan So what could Toby do that would make Eric feel better right now?

Young Man 1 He could fuck the living daylights out of Eric.

Eric Toby is very good at that.

Morgan Yes, but so soon in the story?

The Lads insist: definitely, yes.

Morgan If that's what you need.

End of Scene Two.

SCENE THREE

December, 2015

1. Eric and Toby's Apartment

Toby I spent the entire day writing the same speech over and over. But I think it's good. Would you read it for me?

Eric Yes, of course, I'd love to. But later. I thought we could do something else in the meantime.

Toby Wait, are you naked?

Eric Why don't you join me and find out?

Toby What about dinner?

Eric We can order in.

Toby Yeah but if we wait too long it'll take forever and you know I have to eat by eight / or I won't be able to sleep . . .

Eric Remember that time you told me to meet you at the Whitney in the tightest jeans I owned and no underwear?

Toby I miss the old Whitney.

Eric It was a John Currin exhibition and you kept trying to slide your hands down inside my jeans.

Toby The new one is so far *away*.

Eric My jeans were so tight you couldn't even get your hand in. But you huffed and you puffed and then finally you got your hand down in there.

Toby But I do like the views upstairs.

Eric And then you couldn't get it out.

Toby You were the one who decided to do squats all week.

Eric Oh I *do* have your attention.

Toby You definitely had my attention in those jeans.

Eric I've spent a lot of time at the squat rack this week.

Toby Get over here. That ass needs a face in it.

Morgan Toby undresses and joins Eric in bed.

Toby God, I love your ass. How does a Jewish boy from Westchester end up with an ass this nice? Must be from your mother's side of the family.

Eric Can we not talk about my mother while I have an erection?

Toby You have an erection? I want an erection. How come he has an erection and I don't?

Young Man 1 Eric dives under the covers and starts blowing him.

Eric Here.

Toby Okay! Get me hard, baby.
Oh wow.
Oh yeah.
It's not working.

Eric Think of something sexy.

Toby Remember that time on Fire Island when we watched those two guys fucking in the Meat Rack? That was so hot.

Eric That's working.

Toby Yeah. I wish we'd done that. I really wanted to but you were afraid of ticks. You riding my cock on a sheet in the Meat Rack. Or maybe a quilt. A quilt is thicker. Like my dick in your mouth. Oh yeah, there we go.

Eric Fuck me, Toby.

Toby Yeah, you want me to fuck you?

Eric I just said that I did.

Toby Right. I was just going along with, I . . . right, I'll fuck you like we're in the Meat Rack.

Eric What is with you and the Meat Rack all of a sudden? That was like, / five years ago.

Toby I don't know, I thought it was hot, didn't you?

Eric Yeah, but I haven't been obsessing on it ever since.

Toby I wouldn't say I was obsessing. It just popped into my mind just now is all.

Eric Toby, slide your dick inside me right now.

Toby Yes sir!

Morgan Toby starts to enter Eric.

Toby That okay?

Eric Hold on . . .
   Okay, try again.
   Slowly!

Toby How's that?

Eric There you go. Slowly.

Toby More?

Eric A little.

Morgan Toby slides in more.

Toby Fuck, that feels good.

Eric Okay, more.

Toby 'More' is the rest.

Eric Yeah, go for it.

Morgan Toby slides in all the way. They both moan, feeling good. They fuck slowly.

Toby Wow, you're tight. When was the last time you –

Eric What?

Toby Did you . . . you know . . . hook up with anyone when I took that trip to Chicago last month?

Eric Why? Did you?

Toby This one guy on Grindr.

Eric How was he?

Toby Kinda hot actually. What about you?

Eric Last for me was this guy last fall. I forget where you were.

Toby How was he?

Eric Eh. He fucked me like he was doing me a favor.

Morgan They fuck *silently*.

After a moment:

Toby Should we order Chinese tonight?

Eric We had Chinese last night.

Toby You like Chinese.

Eric Toby, I don't know. Can we talk about this after?

Toby It's just that I'd like to know what we're ordering when we're done so we can get right on it.

Eric Get on my ass, motherfucker.

Toby Yeah, you want my dick, little boy?

Eric Toby, ew.

Toby Sorry.

Eric Fuck me, Toby.

Toby Like that?

Eric Harder.

Toby Like that?

Eric Harder.

Toby I can't really go any / harder.

Eric Fuck me harder.

Toby That feel good?

Eric That feels amazing. I love you, Toby.

Toby Oh God, I'm close already. Shit, I'm sorry.

Eric It's okay, Toby. Come inside me.

God I love you.
I love you.
I love you.
God, I wanna get married.

Toby What?

Eric Oh fuck, nothing. Forget I said that.

Toby You wanna get married?

Eric Bad timing, bad timing. Keep going.

Toby But now it's just out there.

Eric Forget I said anything. Just bring it home, baby.

Morgan Toby starts to bring it home.

Toby Are you thinking like a big fancy wedding?

Eric We don't have to talk about this now.

Toby Oh fuck, I'm getting close.
Oh God.

Eric Yeah.

Toby Oh God.

Eric Yeah.

Toby Oh God.

Eric Yeah.

Morgan Release the hounds!

Toby Oh God!!

After a moment:

Toby You wanna get married?

Eric Forget it.

Toby No, Eric . . . tell me

Eric Yes, Toby. I do. I want to get married and start a family and spend my life with you. I have for a while.

Toby Why didn't you say something before?

Eric Just waiting for the right moment.
    You don't have to answer right away. But I would like to talk about it. I mean, we've been together seven years –

Toby Yeah, fuck it, why not?

Eric We can talk about it another time.

Toby No, I think we should do it. Should we have the party here?

Eric Oh. Well. Actually –

Toby Yeah, you're right: we'll save up for a really nice wedding. Maybe at the Plaza or in Maui.

Eric That's really expensive, babe. It's not like I make a fortune / and –

Toby We'll be able to afford it. Gimme a year. Two at the most. I'm going to finish this play and it's going to get produced and I will finally show people that I'm worthy of their attention. And their respect. And eventually their money. And we will build something real for ourselves, not just borrowed. Something that's ours. How's that sound?

Eric Uh, yeah. Let's do that.

Toby Deal.

Eric Did we just get engaged?

Toby I think we just did.

Eric Holy shit! I've got your cum inside my ass and we just got engaged.

Toby Where's *that* Cole Porter song?

2. *Toby Interlude*

Morgan Why didn't Eric tell Toby about the apartment? Why did he choose to seduce him rather than inform him?

Eric It isn't a certainty yet. And Toby is so focused on writing his play.

Morgan I think there's another reason. One that touches on Toby's nature – perhaps even Toby's past. Let's start with his writing, for it seems to be driving his character.

Young Man 1 Toby has written a novel based on his childhood.

Morgan Excellent. Now, if I may: the book is good –

Toby Thank you.

Morgan – not great. It's engaging, and wittily written. If a touch facile.

Young Man 1 It's published as a young adult novel.

Morgan What's the name of Toby's central character?

Young Man 1 Elan.

Morgan Perfect!

Toby Rich kid, seventeen, raised on the Upper West Side. A twenty-first-century gay Holden Caulfield. Sexy as fuck, sarcastic, rude, yet undeniably compelling. He's basically me.

Morgan Or.
    Elan is everything Toby has always wanted to be. He is who Toby has convinced himself – and the world – that he's become.

Toby Are you saying that Toby's life is a lie?

Morgan I'm saying that the truth is something he has spent his life running from.

Toby That doesn't sound very fun.

Morgan It isn't. Springtime. New York City Ballet. A rainstorm.

End of Scene Three.

SCENE FOUR

Spring and Summer 2016

1. Lincoln Center

A heavy rainstorm. Toby stands under the massive eaves, dressed in a smart suit. A large, expensive umbrella in his hand.
   Young Man 1 emerges from the lobby.

Young Man 1 Toby? You're Toby, right? Toby Darling?

Toby Hey, thanks for reading. I'm sorry I don't have a pen on me.

Young Man 1 No, we met maybe six months ago. At your apartment? We had each other's bags.

Toby Oh yeah. The little kleptomaniac.

Young Man 1 Hey, you took *my* bag. I'm Adam Lucas McDowell.

Toby Oh, the full name. In that case, I'm Toby Michael Darling.

Adam You look . . . wow.

Toby Aw, thanks. I was going for 'wow.' You usually dress like that for the ballet?

Adam Oh. No, I grabbed a rush ticket spur of the moment. Is your boyfriend with you?

Toby Eric ended up working late tonight. Beautiful second-tier seat gone to waste.

Adam I was all the way in the back.

Toby Well, someone has to be. What'd you think?

Adam Oh, of the program? Really good. I loved the new piece most especially.

Toby Yeah. Life-changing, in fact.

Adam Oh! Speaking of life-changing, I read your book.

Toby Get out.

Adam I really loved it. So vivid, so fully realized. Like Salinger, almost.

Toby 'Almost'? What do you mean / 'almost'?

Adam Oh. I just mean, you know, Salinger's one of the greatest American writers / of all time and –

Toby I'm just fucking with you.

Adam Your character Elan is so vibrant. He pops, you know? I know that kid. I grew up with that kid.

Toby The snobby gay rich kid?

Adam He's not snobby, he's just particular.

Toby That's what I always say!

Adam Well I loved it. And I'm glad I got a chance to tell you.

The rain intensifies.

Toby Do you have an umbrella?

Adam I thought I did.

Toby I can walk you to the train.

Adam I actually live not too far from here.

Morgan Do you? Where?

Adam Oh. Over on 74th Street?

Toby And what?

Adam Riverside?

Toby What, like with a dozen roommates or something?

Adam No, I live with my parents.

Toby Oh . . .

Adam Yeah, so. I don't mind / walking in the rain.

Toby Nonsense. It's pouring out. You'll catch your death.

Morgan They huddled together under Toby's umbrella and headed out into the monsoon. Eventually they arrived at Adam's apartment, which was . . .

Young Man 1 Oh. A five-bedroom, six-and-a-half-bathroom with park and river views that took up half of the 11th floor of a majestic neo-Georgian building. For you see: Adam Lucas McDowell was filthy stinkin' rich.

2. *Adam's Apartment*

Toby Oh wow.

Adam You can come in if you want.

Toby I don't want to bother your parents.

Adam They're in Japan right now. My dad has scotch, if you want. Like really old scotch.

Toby How old is 'really old'? Like from the Clinton administration?

Adam No, like from the Treaty of Versailles.

Toby Uh, yeah, I'll have a glass.

Adam pours Toby a drink.

This place is amazing.

Adam It's just my home, no biggie.
Here you go.

Toby sips.

Toby Dear God.

Adam Is it okay?

Toby Baby, you've just handed me the last century of world history distilled into spirit form. It's a quintillion times better than okay.

Morgan Toby moved over to the massive bookcase. There on the shelf – in front of what looked like a priceless first edition of *The Great Gatsby* – was a photograph of Adam with the President and his wife, taken inside that very room.

Toby Toby sipped the scotch, knowing that each swallow was worth more than what he currently had in his checking account. (*To Adam.*) How do you know the Obamas?

Adam My mom went to law school with him. It broke her heart when I decided to go to Yale.

Toby Yes, I'm sure that's every mother's nightmare.

Adam Did you go to grad school for writing?

Toby I didn't study writing in grad school.

Morgan A clever dodge, a linguistic sleight of hand: Toby hadn't even finished high school.

Toby Are you still in school?

Adam No, I graduated in the spring.

Toby So what do you do now?

Adam I'm an actor.

Toby Of course you are.

Adam Where did you go / to school?

Toby Any luck so far? With the acting?

Adam I get called back a lot. Haven't booked a real job yet but there are a few agents and managers I've been talking to.

Toby Not bad for your first year.

Adam I've got friends on Broadway already.

Toby And I'm sure you're just sooo happy for them.

Adam I am. It's just, you know . . .

Toby 'When's it gonna be my turn?'

Adam Yeah. It's like such a struggle sometimes.

Toby What the fuck do you know about struggle, rich boy? Some of us had to work our asses off to become the mediocrities that we are today. Brave choice, rich boy. Go be an artist. You're the only ones who can afford to anymore.

Morgan But what Toby actually said was:

Toby Keep struggling, Adam. It'll be worth it in the end.

Adam Thank you. It's exciting that you're adapting your book for theatre. Do you know what's happening with it?

Toby Actually I do. My agent's good friends with the director Tom Durrell. Do you know him?

Adam No, should I?

Toby Oh yes, Adam, you absolutely should. He's a genius. Anyway, Tom read my play and really flipped for it. We've been developing it and workshopping it all winter long and we go into production in Chicago this September.

Adam What does Elan look like? You don't give a lot of physical details in the book. Is that on purpose?

Toby So every boy who reads it can believe that they're him.

Adam That's exactly the experience I had! I'm convinced he looks like me.

Toby Maybe he does.

Morgan It's stopped raining.

Toby I should go.

Adam Would you sign my copy first?

Toby Yeah, of course.

Morgan 'To Adam, whom I hope to be when I grow up.'

Adam Thank you.

Toby Hey, how'd you like to come have dinner at our place next week?

Adam Really? Yeah, I'd love that!

Toby Great. I know Eric would love to see you again.

Morgan Toby left, forgetting his umbrella. Adam picked it up and saw its condition. It had all gone along the seams and been re-patched. In truth, it was an appalling umbrella. But from a distance it was dazzling. Like its owner, it did not bear close scrutiny.

As he rode the wood-paneled elevator down to the lobby, Toby thought . . .

Toby Who the fuck is that kid? Boy, did he bury the lead that first time we met him.

Morgan What was he going to say? 'Hi, I'm Adam and I'm a child of privilege?'

Toby Yes! I'd have cards printed up, I'd have T-shirts made!

Morgan A week later, Adam walked twenty blocks north and joined Eric and Toby for dinner.

3. *Eric and Toby's Apartment*

Eric What do you mean you've never seen a Truffaut film?

Toby Okay, calm down. He's only twenty-one.

Eric But he grew up in Manhattan!

Adam My parents aren't really into movies. We did see a Broadway show every Thanksgiving.

Eric Okay, so let's start there. What's your favorite play of all time?

Adam *Mamma Mia!*

Eric Let's start with movies instead. Can we assume that if it's in black-and-white you haven't seen it?

Adam Yes.

Eric Great. We should start with the French New Wave. *Jules et Jim* or maybe *The 400 Blows*.

Toby Don't get too excited, it is not a movie about blowjobs.

Eric Better yet: what's something you've never seen that you've always been curious about? There's no wrong answer.

Adam Well. I've always wanted to see *The Deer Hunter*.

44

Eric and Toby look at each other.

Eric Oh. *The Deer Hunter*.

Toby I mean, it's a classic.

Eric Great cast.

Toby Epic sweep.

Eric Meryl Streep.

Toby Eric . . .

Eric Fuck it. Let's watch *The Deer Hunter*.

Adam No, we don't have to / watch it tonight.

Eric When broadening our horizons, the word 'no' is not in our vocabulary.

Toby Unless Eric thinks your taste is for shit.

Morgan And so they watched *The Deer Hunter*. Adam returned the next night for –

Young Man 7 *Breathless*.

Morgan And then the next night for –

Young Man 2 *Jules et Jim*.

Morgan Eric and Toby took Adam under their wings that spring and early summer, folding him into their lives as if he had always been there. Adam found himself at Eric and Toby's with increasing frequency, even going so far as to leave some clothes in their guest bedroom.

Young Man 1 A fondness and an intimacy grew between them – a kind that Adam had never experienced before with older gay men.

Eric Older?!

Toby Fuck you, kid!

Young Man 1 It was, in fact, the first adult friendship of Adam's life.

Morgan Eric delighted in filling in the gaps in Adam's cultural education, making regular visits with him to –

Young Man 5 – Film Forum –

Young Man 6 – and MOMA.

Young Man 8 They visited the Delacorte –

Young Man 3 – went for day trips to Jacob Riis Beach –

Young Man 4 – and hiking in Bear Mountain.

Toby Toby participated in these events but not as often and always at a remove. He spent most of that summer feverishly rewriting his play.

4. *Adam and Eric*

Adam Do you think Toby would let me audition for his play?

Eric You should ask him!

Adam I was hoping you'd ask him for me. I'm not sure how Toby feels about me.

Eric Toby adores you.

Adam Toby intimidates me.

Eric Toby is very fond of you.

Adam Still, would you talk to him for me?

5. *Eric and Toby*

Toby Waste of time.

Eric How much time could it possibly take? It's one audition.

Toby He isn't even a trained actor. He's got a BA in blowjobs from Yale.

Eric If he's not right, you send him home, that's the end of it. Would you at least talk to him?

6. *Toby and Adam*

Toby First of all, next time you want a favor from me, you ask me and not Eric, okay?

Adam I didn't want to bother you.

Toby Second of all, you're not going to get far in this business if you're afraid of bothering people. Now, do you want to audition for my play?

Adam Yes.

Toby Why?

Adam It's a great part.

Toby No shit. Is that the only reason?

Adam I want to prove myself to you.

Toby Me? Why me?

Adam Because I admire you, Toby.

Toby is completely taken aback, then regroups.

Toby The role is Everest.

Young Man 3 Oh boy.

Toby Elan never leaves the stage the entire play. He has more lines than Hamlet.

47

Young Man 7 Really, Toby? Hamlet?

Toby Shut up. (*To Adam.*) Think you're up to it?

Adam Yes.

Toby Okay, then.

7. *Toby and Eric*

Morgan And so Adam auditioned for Toby's play and, to Toby's great astonishment, it was as if Adam became Elan right there in the room.

Toby Jesus –
      That kid is really special, Eric.

Eric Yeah, babe. I've been telling you that for weeks now.

Toby I mean as an actor. Or at least as this character. It's kind of perfect, when you think about it. Adam's this spoiled little rich kid.

Eric Adam isn't spoiled.

Toby I just mean he and Elan have had similar upbringings.

Eric They're very different people, Toby.

Toby What do you know? Elan is my character.

Eric And Adam's my friend.

Toby He's my friend, too.

Eric So be nicer to him.

Toby I may be giving him his first professional job, for Chrissake. How much nicer can I be? Let's just pray he doesn't fuck it up.

8. *Eric and Adam*

Adam When did you know Toby was the man you wanted to marry?

Eric Well, I think if I was honest, I'd say it was the night I first met him. The next seven years was basically due diligence. But remember: when Toby and I met – and certainly when we were growing up – marriage wasn't an option for us. I just knew he was someone I could spend my life with. Are you thinking about proposing to someone?

Adam Oh my God, no. I'm just curious about your relationship. Who proposed to who?

Morgan Eric proposed to Toby.

Adam Did you get down on one knee?

Eric I was kind of on both knees at the time.

Adam Are you and Toby going to have children?

Eric I'd love to have children. I've always dreamed of it.

Morgan But of course, Toby had a difficult childhood.

Toby What?

Eric I don't even know the whole story.

Morgan Toby's parents died when he was young.

Toby Morgan.

Adam I didn't know that.

Eric I only really know the contours of Toby's story.

Morgan He moved to New York when he was seventeen.

Toby Hold on.

Adam I thought he was raised in New York.

Eric That's a complicated history.

Toby Please stop.

Eric He doesn't talk about his past – not even to me.

Adam Does that bother you?

Eric It used to. But Toby has let me know him in ways he won't let others. I've learned to understand what love looks like to him.

Adam What does love look like to *you*?

Eric Taking care of Toby, I guess. Because no one ever has.

Adam Do you and Toby still have sex?

Morgan Yes, they do.

Adam Do you . . . ever have sex with other people?

Eric Let's just say there's a difference between monogamy and monotony.

Adam Would you and Toby ever want to have sex with me?

Toby Say yes.

Eric Oh.

Adam I'm sorry.

Toby Say yes.

Eric No. No, don't be sorry.

Toby Just say yes, we'll figure out the details later.

Eric That is a very flattering and tempting offer.

Toby And so . . .

Adam You don't / have to –

Eric No, truly. You're very attractive.

Toby He's hot as fuck.

Eric And under different circumstances I would be all over that.

Toby Yeah, baby.

Eric Or under that.

Toby Yeah, baby.

Eric Whichever you prefer.

Toby Yeah, baby!

Eric But here's why I think it might not be a good idea: if you were to get the job in Toby's play, I think you don't want that energy between you as you work.

Toby What?!

Eric And if you don't get that job . . . well, maybe this friendship is about something different. In other words: let's not go and fuck up a good thing.

Toby You're killing me, Eric.

Adam Yes. Yes, you're right. I'm sorry.

Eric Do not apologize.

Adam I don't really know what I'm doing.

Eric You seem to be doing just fine.

Adam Could I . . . come to you sometimes for direction? Advice? For wisdom?

Eric You want wisdom . . . from me?

Adam Yes. Very much.

Eric Oh. Well.

Morgan How about a little perspective instead?

Eric For whatever that's worth.

Adam Yes. Perspective. I'd love that. Thank you, Eric.

Morgan Eric had never been solicited both for sex and for wisdom in the same conversation. For all of his life, he'd been someone's son, younger brother, or student. There had always been someone in front of him to look up to. It had never occurred to him that eventually there'd be someone behind him, looking up to him.

Eric Adam's request made Eric feel valued – perhaps even important – in a way he had never felt before.

Young Man 3 I'm sorry – can I ask another question?

Morgan Of course.

Young Man 3 Earlier you said Eric wasn't special. Do you really think that's true?

Young Man 1 Morgan said Eric didn't *think* he was special.

Young Man 3 But how can he possibly think that? He seems pretty remarkable to me.

Morgan You've just stumbled across a great secret that not even Eric knows. Eric Glass was wrong about himself in every imaginable way. Not only was he the bravest person he knew, he also possessed the ability to change the world to an extent far greater than he could possibly imagine. Eric Glass's entire conception of himself was false. He simply didn't know it yet.

Eric How will he learn?

Morgan Heartbreak.

9. *Eric, Toby and Adam*

Morgan So: does Adam get the job?

The Lads really want him to. All eyes on Toby.

Toby Yeah, fuck it! Let's give him the job.

The Lads celebrate.

Adam I can't believe this is happening! I really want to do an amazing job for you, Toby.

Toby You'd fucking better, kid.

Adam I will, I promise. Oh shit, this is real, isn't it? I'm going to be playing this part. Who else is going to be in it? I have some friends I could recommend for the ensemble. Do you know where your apartment is going to be in Chicago? Maybe we can take yoga classes together. I'm going to be off-book from day one.

Morgan Toby led Adam out onto the terrace and before Eric could join them, the door closed, creating a separation between them. Eric watched on the other side of the plate glass window as Toby and Adam hugged and laughed and daydreamed together.

End of Scene Four.

SCENE FIVE

Autumn 2016

Young Man 7 Toby and Adam left for Chicago after Labor Day, leaving Eric by himself.

Young Man 8 Eric almost instantly became lonely.

Young Man 4 For the first time in years, his beloved home was quiet.

Young Man 1 And then one morning, a chance encounter with an old friend upended not just his silence, but also his life.

Young Man 4 The reunion occurred, of all places, on Eric's elevator.

Eric Walter? My goodness, hello.

Walter Eric Glass?

Eric Are you visiting someone in the building?

Walter No, Henry and I are subletting for a few months while our new place is being renovated.

Eric Stop. Toby and I live on the 15th floor.

Walter Imagine that.

Eric Listen, Walter: I feel really bad about ghosting on you like I did last year.

Walter 'Ghosting'?

Eric Falling off the face of the earth after Toby . . . well, you know . . .

Walter I told you to put that out of your mind.

Eric Yes, I know you did but . . . well, I wasn't sure if you'd put it out of *yours*. And so I just . . . well, I didn't handle it well. And I'm sorry.

Walter Apology accepted. Now / if you don't mind –

Eric I'd love to invite you and Henry over for dinner one night.

Walter Henry's in London through Thanksgiving.

Eric Oh. Toby's in Chicago. I guess we're both on our own this autumn.

Walter Yes, it seems we are.

Young Man 2 A week later, Eric slipped a note under Walter's door:

Eric 'Walter, if you're up for it, I'd love to invite you over for dinner tomorrow. Stop by around seven if you'd like. Apartment 15A. Eric.'

Young Man 3 The doorbell rang at seven sharp.

Eric Please, come in.

Young Man 6 There was a frailty to Walter that was new.

Young Man 2 What had once been a distant, inscrutable aspect was now positively spectral.

Young Man 4 Eric instinctively put his hand on Walter's back as if to steady him as he passed. The older man shrugged off the gesture without a word.

Eric You know, I think this is the first time you and I have ever been alone together.

Walter That can't be true.

Eric I think it is. What if we discover that Henry and Toby are the interesting ones and that you and I actually have nothing to say to each other?

Walter That's what alcohol is for.

Eric Would you like a glass of wine?

Walter I'm fine, thank you. Your apartment is enormous.

Eric Oh, yes. How long have you and Henry been together?

Walter Oh. Almost thirty-six years.

Eric That's amazing.

Walter There isn't all that much to it, really. Just a succession of dinners.

Eric I wish I knew Henry better.

Walter After thirty-six years I don't feel I completely know him.

Eric I feel the same way about Toby. Oh! Toby and I are getting married next year.

Walter Really? Congratulations.

Eric Thank you.

Walter I've always had the impression that you and Toby were ill-matched.

Eric Oh.

Walter That came out wrong.

Eric There's a right way to say that?

Walter Some relationships thrive on tension.

Eric I wouldn't say we were always in tension.

Walter Opposition maybe.

Eric I think we get along just fine.

Walter You know, I think I will have some wine after all.

Eric pours two glasses of wine.

How big *is* your apartment?

Eric Three bedrooms, two baths. All the other units in the building have been divided and subdivided over the years, turned into condos. This is the only rental unit left in the building.

Walter You rent this apartment?

Eric God yes, I couldn't afford to own this. It's rent-controlled. I only pay five hundred and seventy-five dollars a month for all of this.

Young Man 2 ⎤	What?!
Young Man 6 ⎥	Five hundred and seventy-five dollars!
Young Man 8 ⎥	Fuck you!
Young Man 4 ⎦	I mean, Jesus!

Eric My father took his first steps right over there. My mother was sitting in that very chair when my father proposed to her. I don't think I've spent a Thanksgiving or a Passover anywhere else.

Walter I envy you that.

Eric Don't. Our Seders are endless.

Walter No, I mean the connection to your family's history through your family's home. To live in the same place your father was raised – that's pretty remarkable, Eric. It must inform so much of your life.

Eric grows quiet.

I said something wrong again, didn't I?

Eric The truth is I'm probably going to be evicted at the end of the year.

Walter Evicted? Oh. I'm sorry. On what grounds?

Eric The lease is ironclad. If my grandmother isn't in residence for more than a year, they can call the whole thing off.

Walter Where does she live now?

Eric In that urn on the mantel over there.
    I mean, technically she's still in residence but I don't think they see it that way.
    My parents are fighting it, but . . . things aren't looking good. If I look on the bright side, I think it might be exciting to start a new chapter in my life. But it won't be

this place and it won't have this history. But at least I'll have Toby.

I decided to befriend you and Henry because I thought: 'That's going to be me and Toby someday. I'd better study how they did it.'

Walter The truth is I'm bad at new relationships. Henry travels so much. We're always in a new city, and never long enough to put down roots.

Eric That must be hard.

Walter Part of the bargain.

Eric You think of your relationship as a 'bargain'? I'm sorry. That was rude. Don't answer that.

Walter Every relationship in Henry's life is a kind of bargain. Henry is a businessman and therefore sees the world exclusively in those terms. He cares most about the things he can use. Money, supremely useful. Intellect, fairly useful. People, intermittently useful. Sentiment, not the least bit useful. I do not subscribe to this view. But that is who Henry is.

Eric And who are you?

Walter Me?
I'm the man who fell in love with Henry Wilcox.

Henry was born in Ohio, in the late 1950s. He was a star of track and field. First in his class and President of the student body association. As American as an Aaron Copland symphony. He married Patricia Fitzgerald while still in college.

Eric Wait, what?

Walter Oh yes. Two sons arrived soon after and Henry was on his way to a life of success and diligence and robust Episcopalianism. And if strapping, ascendant

58

young men with bright futures and beautiful families had secret desires and shameful urges, they hid them from the world, from themselves. Henry worked hard, kept his head down and his hands to himself. Eventually his hard work led him out of the Midwest and into the heart of American business as well as the heart of American temptation: New York City. The Wilcox Family arrived on July 3, 1981. The same summer that I arrived.

Like so many before me, I arrived in New York a refugee from a home that had grown hostile to my presence. I was aware from an early age that I made people uncomfortable. I was moony and effeminate. But small towns have the peculiar habit of tolerating their feathery, delicate boys. But, once I grew older, my parents sent me to ministers, to doctors, to fitness instructors even. Every walk through town felt dangerous, every school day possessed the potential for violence. I would steal my mother's sleeping pills, hoarding them, planning my suicide. I would stare at them nightly, holding them in my hands until one night, perilously close to swallowing them, I was struck by the realization that I didn't want to change, and that what I hated was not my nature, but rather my circumstances. And so I left . . . to seek not my fame and certainly not my fortune, but rather – and rather simply – my dignity.

The only place I knew to go was New York. I had read about the events of June 1969. It was the only place in the world I knew to look for young men like me.

Imagine me at nineteen years old in the middle of Times Square in 1981, my mother's old Samsonite suitcase in my hands, asking strangers for directions to the Stonewall Inn.

Eventually I was given directions by a very friendly pimp.

I rode the graffiti-covered subway downtown, gripping my suitcase so tightly that blisters formed on my hands.

I made my way to the fabled Stonewall Inn only to discover that it has become . . . a Chinese Restaurant.

You can imagine my disappointment.

But I was very hungry. And I'd never eaten Chinese food before. So I stayed in Mr Shun's Dim Sum Emporium and I knew that I had made the right decision.

Henry, meanwhile, is not so certain. He's twenty-four and already the father of two young boys, earning more money in a month than most men twice his age make in a year. He owns a four-bedroom house in White Plains and he commutes daily to his office downtown. There's Henry, knocking back after-work martinis with his colleagues. There's Henry in the steam room at the East Side Club. There's Henry on the 11:30 train headed home to his family. There's Henry in the shower, remorseful and penitent, attempting to expunge his great secret from his skin. There's Henry sliding into bed at one in the morning next to a wife who suspects more than she lets on.

We meet at a rooftop party overlooking Christopher Street. Henry's rented an apartment in the city while his family spends its summer in Montauk. I notice him first and am thunderstruck by the sight of him. Honey chestnut hair worn slightly long as was the style of the day. Well-developed chest threatening the integrity of the polo shirt he's wearing. I move into his line of sight and wait to be noticed. It doesn't take long. We chat for as long as we can stand to, then head back to his apartment and his bed.

Henry was the first, the only man I ever loved. No, that's a blatant lie and shame on me for telling it. Henry Wilcox was the only man I ever needed to be loved by. It was in Henry's gaze, from his kisses and through his touch that I finally glimpsed my own worth. I fell hard into Henry's handsomeness, his intelligence, his potential . . . no, not his potential – his certainty.

I was never meant to be Henry's life partner. I was the person he was dancing with when the music stopped. By that point, whispers of disease had graduated to rumors. Rumors became stories. And stories became fact. Henry had arrived at the party just in time for it to end.

For five years, Henry and I clung to one another for safety, for comfort, as the city burned around us. By the summer of 1987, we had had enough of funerals and hospital visits and the sight of thousands of once vital men laid to waste. We decided to look for a house as far from civilization as we could find. We finally stumbled across a rambling old farmhouse on an aimless country road, three hours north of here, built in the late eighteenth century. It's set off from the road so you have the illusion of being alone in the world. And in front of the house, my favorite thing on the property: an enormous cherry tree that has been there since the time George Washington was out terrorizing them. It puts on the most astonishing show twice a year. In the autumn, it burns deep orange and red leaves, as if the tree were on fire. And in the spring, vibrant blushing flowers which eventually fall ever so gently to the ground in a kind of aerial ballet.

And – I don't know if you'll believe me but it's true – deep in the trunk of the tree are a set of pig's teeth that were put there I don't know how many generations ago. The superstition among the colonials was that if you bite the bark of the tree, it will cure all your ailments.

Eric And does it?

Walter No. Of course it doesn't. Pure superstition. And yet, there in the country, on rolling pastureland, with flowers and breezes and cherry trees with pig's teeth stuck in the bark, there was no death, there was no illness, there was no loss or danger. Henry bought it the next day and we lived there for a year without ever leaving the area. We cooked, we gardened, we read underneath the cherry tree. And we avoided all news from our friends, from the outside world.

After a year, Henry grew restless. He began traveling to London to start the first of his many ventures that would eventually make him a very wealthy man. Without him, I began to stew – and so early one morning I decided to return to the city. I hadn't been there in over a year. I was terrified of what I might find. I was about to take myself to lunch when I ran into an old friend of ours. Peter West was his name. Dear Peter. Darling man, more clever than anyone I ever knew. And handsome as sin. I wouldn't have recognized him if he hadn't called out to me from across Fifth Avenue. Peter had 'the look', the telltale sign that someone was infected. His handsome face was sunken and sallow, his muscles had melted away. It was clear in one glance that he had it. He was also, I discovered, essentially homeless. His landlord evicted him. He'd been estranged from his family for years. He had nowhere to go. We took the next train upstate and phoned for a cab. The driver took one look at Peter and fled. We stood there, four miles from my house with no other means to get there but our legs. The day was beautiful and Peter smiled as he breathed in the country air through his rattling lungs. The sun was setting as we approached the house. I could feel a release in Peter's body. I put him in one of the rooms upstairs. Peter spent the next five days slowly dying. I cleaned him when he fouled himself. I held him as he wept in grief. I comforted him as he screamed in pain. I had no idea I had such strength. On Peter's fourth day, Henry returned from London. When I told him that Peter was upstairs, Henry flew into a rage, accusing me of betrayal, of bringing the plague into our home. I had never seen such fear on a man's face as I saw in Henry's that day. He got back into his car and drove away. Peter died as the sun was rising his fifth day with us. Henry returned to

London, leaving me alone for several months without so much as a phone call. I spent the first few weeks of my exile wondering if I was wrong to show such kindness to a friend. But, oh Eric, to see Peter's ravaged face, and to look into those frightened eyes, I believe that if I had left Peter on that sidewalk, returning to my place of peace without him, I would have ruined that house for myself far more than I ever could have ruined it for Henry. I eventually came to see that leaving the city and our friends behind was as unforgivable an act of cowardice as I have ever performed. The answer, I realized, was not to shut the world out but rather to fling the doors open and to invite it in. And so, while Henry's furious silence roared at me from across the Atlantic, I brought others in their last days up to the house. I replayed that scene over and over with friends, acquaintances and eventually strangers. One by one they came to my house, and one by one they died there.

After several months, Henry had his lawyers draw up the paperwork to name me the sole owner of the house. Peter West is the reason that house became my property. It would not be the blessed place that it is if it had not first hosted Peter's torture and his death. Henry cannot see it that way and that is Henry's to sort out. I think that even after thirty-six years, Henry and I are still sorting it out. If it is ever to be sorted.

Silence.

Eric I can't imagine what those years were like. I don't even know how to . . .

I can *understand* what it was. But I cannot possibly *feel* what it was.

Walter Tell me the name of one of your closest friends.

Eric Tristan.

Walter Imagine that Tristan is dead. Name another.

Eric Jasper.

Walter Jasper is also dead.

Eric Jason.

Walter Jason has been at St Vincent's for two weeks. The toxoplasmosis has left him with dementia.

Eric Jason, his husband.

Walter Because they cannot legally be married, abandonment is simpler. Jason has left him.

Young Men (*variously*)

Patrick is dead.

Alex is dead.

Colin is dead.

Lucas is infected.

Zach is dying from pneumocystis carinii.

Chris is healthy.

His partner has just been diagnosed.

You just visited Mark in the hospital. Tonight you will visit Will.

Eddie's funeral is tomorrow.

Michael's body is covered with KS lesions.

Jeffrey is infected but asymptomatic.

Sati is dead.

Daniel is infected.

Stephen is infected.

Brian's partner has peripheral neuropathy. He screams in pain at the slightest touch.

Scott is in Paris, hoping to get HPA-23.

Javier went home to die in his mother's house.

Jonathan's family won't take him back.

Brandon is dead.

Matthew is dead.

Leo is infected.

Kurt is infected but he doesn't know it.

David, his partner, will find out first.

Frankie's sister calls you to tell you he's died.

Adam has disappeared altogether.

Phillip is dead.

Trevor is dead.

Kevin is infected.

Walter Rumors fly about incarcerations of gay men as a precaution.

Young Men (*variously*)

Politicians begin to openly discuss mass quarantines.

There is talk of outlawing homosexuality, rumors of deportations.

Anti-gay violence is on the rise.

The American public becomes galvanized by the epidemic: not against the illness but against the people who have it.

Businesses cancel health insurance policies for employees with AIDS.

Walter States pass legislation requiring home sellers to divulge if a Person with AIDS has ever lived there.

Young Men (*variously*)

Sam is dead.

Mark is dead.

Miguel is infected.

Paul has it.

Ben has it.

Carlos has it.

Wesley is dead.

Caleb is dead.

David is dead.

James is dead.

Andrew is dead.

Jacob is dead.

Walter That is what it was.

End of Act One.

Act Two

SCENE ONE

1. Chicago Club / Eric and Toby's Apartment

Thumping house music. A group of men dancing. Toby is in the middle of them. So is Adam. Toby's phone vibrates in his pocket. He looks at it, makes his way off the floor.

Toby Fair warning: I'm drunk and stoned and I also might be rolling.

Eric Oh my God, Toby. One drug at a time!

Toby Tom gave us each a Molly. The man's a fucking CVS. Hi!

Eric Yes, you are. I'm two minutes away from turning thirty-four.

Toby It's only eleven.

Eric Time zones, baby. You're an hour behind in Chicago.

Toby Oh, right! I set a reminder for midnight. I woulda called too late. Or too early? Ugh, math!

Eric Where are you?

Toby A bunch of us decided to go out dancing.

Eric Is Adam with you?

Toby He is!

Eric Give him a big hug for me.

Toby Will do!

67

Eric Are you taking care of him?

Toby He's not a child, Eric.

Eric He's younger than he thinks.

Toby What are you doing tomorrow? Anything fun?

Eric The Lads are coming over for brunch. I'm introducing them to Walter.

Toby You and Walter seem to be spending a lot of time together. Should I be jealous?

Eric Yes, very. He's had quite a life.

Toby Listen, it's chilly out and I'm scantily clad. I'll call you tomorrow, okay?

Eric Okay. I love you, Toby.

Toby Yeah, me too, babe. Byeeee! Happy birthday!

He hangs up and returns to the club and dives back into the middle of the crowd.

2. Adam's Apartment in Chicago

Adam Fuck, I'm still rolling.

Toby You can't still be rolling.

Adam Your eyes are so beautiful.

Toby Wow, you're still rolling.

Adam I love you, Toby.

Toby That's my cue to go.

Adam No, let's stay up and talk.

Toby It's four-thirty in the morning.

Adam goes into the bathroom.

68

Toby You're not about to throw up, are you?

Adam I think I have to pee.

The shower starts offstage.

Toby Are you taking a shower?

Adam (*off*) What?

Toby Are you taking a shower?

Adam (*off*) I'm going to take a quick shower.

Toby I think it's sweet that you brought a framed photo of you and your parents.

Adam (*off*) What?

Toby Can you even hear me right now?

Adam (*off*) What?

Toby Then I'll only say this once: I think you're really amazing.

Adam (*off*) I can't hear a word you're saying, Toby.

Toby Good.

Watching you rehearse these last few weeks, to see Elan come to life in that room, to watch you become him . . . You're so very good in this play, Adam . . . and in the few more moments that I can say these things, I just want you to know that you amaze me, Adam. And I really wanna fuck you right now.

The shower stops. Adam enters with a towel wrapped around his waist.

Adam I wanna ask you something.

Toby Okay . . .

Adam How am I doing? In the part, I mean. As Elan.

Toby It's early days.

Adam I can't get a firm grip on him at times, you know what I mean?

Toby You're still figuring him out.

Adam I mean, he's kind of a dick, you know? And I love that about him. But he can be a little cocky and manipulative.

Toby Right.

Adam So . . . I dunno. I just don't want the audience not to like me.

Toby Trust me, Adam. The audience is going to like you. I wouldn't overthink it. Just remember he ain't no virgin.

Adam Have I been playing him like a virgin?

Toby Touched for the very first time.

Adam You don't think *I'm* a virgin, do you?

Toby God, I hope you're not.

Adam Far from it.

Toby Oh 'far', huh? How far, exactly?

Adam You mean in years or in . . .?

Toby Cocks. How far from virginity are you in erect penises? If you lined them up end to end, how far to the moon could you get?

Adam Probably not as far as you. I guess you've had a lot of sex in your life, huh?

Toby I'm Cape fuckin' Canaveral, baby.

Adam You're probably more like Elan in that regard than I am.

Adam removes the towel, standing before Toby naked.

Toby Here's what I'll say: if Elan stepped out of the shower and stood before me completely naked, he wouldn't then pussyfoot around about what he wanted, he'd just come right out and say it. That, I think, is the main difference between you and the character that I've written. I should get to bed.

A moment, then Adam puts on underwear.

We need to take you shopping for better underwear.

Adam What's wrong with my underwear?

Toby It looks like you bought it at Costco.

Adam But . . . I did.

Toby Gay men shouldn't shop at Costco until they're at least forty and own land. What if you'd hooked up tonight? You really want a guy seeing you in that Fruit-of-the-Loom banality you're wearing right now?

Adam Why do you always pick on me?

Toby 'Why do you always pick on me?' I tease you, there's a difference.

Adam Why can't you just be nice to me?

Toby I *am* nice to you.

Adam You're always making fun of how rich and spoiled I am. Sometimes I think you don't like me.

Toby Oh come on, Adam. Don't be such a baby.

Adam I'm not a baby. Stop calling me that.

Toby You have to know that you've lived a pretty protected life.

Adam Is that my fault?

Toby No, not at all. But I hope you realize it's, like, a one-in-a-million life you're living.

Adam I know I'm very fortunate.

Toby I'm hard on you because someone needs to be. You can't expect the world to coddle you the way Mommy does. You can't expect to get what you want just because you want it. You can't coast through life without some kind of adversity.

Adam You know I was adopted, right?

Toby Oh shut up, you were not.
  Were you?

Adam I was born in Texas. My mother was sixteen. She left me at the hospital. My parents adopted me when I was two weeks old.

Toby Adam, I'm sorry. It's a one-in-a-*billion* life you're living.

Adam Fuck you, Toby.

Toby That's the spirit.

Adam Why can't you encourage me?

Toby Because you get enough of that in your life.

Adam But I want it from you.

Toby It bothers me when privileged people pretend that they know what it's like to struggle or be scared to death. So good night, Adam.

Adam I once got fucked in a bathhouse in Prague.

Toby You did not.

Adam Okay then, I didn't.

Morgan Did you?

Toby Oh, I see: is this your way of proving to me that you're not a virgin? I didn't really think / that you were.

Adam I went to Prague over Christmas break my senior year. My boyfriend and I had just broken up, I felt a little lost and heartbroken and so I booked a flight and went.

Toby And what, pray tell, did you do while mending your broken widdle heart in Prague?

Adam I went to museums. I drank in cafés and smoked way too many cigarettes. Then one night I worked up the courage to go to a bathhouse, just to see what it was like.

Morgan What *was* it like?

Adam It was hot.

Toby Oh, come on. If you're going to tell a writer about a visit to a Czech bathhouse, you should at least do him the courtesy of using better adjectives.

Adam My heart pounds in my chest as I ride the metro there from my hotel. My hands tremble with fear as I present / my ID at the door.

Toby Get to the good stuff. If there isn't a dick in your mouth in the next minute, I'm leaving.

Adam I found a hot tub that's empty and I get in.

Toby Okay, so you're in the tub . . .

Adam And this one guy comes over and gets into the tub with me. He reaches down and grabs my dick. I let him stroke me off for a while but I'm not really into it so I get up and leave.

Toby The bathhouse?

Adam No, just the room. I go downstairs into this dark, warm, tiled room. It's basically a long hallway with stalls on either side. The first thing I notice is the sound of moaning. I start to walk down the corridor, passing each stall. Some are empty. Some have one or a couple of guys jerking off or sucking each other off. I remove my towel and walk down the corridor, looking into each of the stalls as I go.

Toby Were you hard?

Adam The hardest.

Toby Did anybody notice you?

Adam Some look up as I pass.

Toby Where did you go then?

Adam I get to this one stall and I find these two guys fucking. I stand there and watch. I'd never seen two people having sex before outside of porn. They both smile and invite me over.

Toby And what happened?

Adam The guy getting fucked starts sucking me off.

Toby Wow. Really?

Adam Then the guy who was fucking him pulls out and joins him.

Toby They're both sucking you off?

Adam Yeah. Back and forth. Both mouths on me at once. Their hands are all over me. I look up and see three other guys in the entryway, watching.

Toby What did you do?

Adam I invite them over.

Toby You did not.

Adam They start feeling my body. They take turns sucking me off. More guys start to show up.

Toby How many?

Adam Eventually? Maybe fifteen, twenty?

Toby You're making this up.

Adam Am I?

Toby Are you?
  Go on.

Adam They're all sucking me off, rubbing my body, eating me out, kissing me all over. They're all exploring me, feeling me. Worshipping me.

Toby How did that feel?

Adam I felt like the most desirable person in the world. I felt like a god.
  Then there's this one guy. So hot, all muscle. He whispers something into my ear. I just smile and nod. Then before I knew what was happening, he slides inside me and starts to fuck me.

Toby Stop it.
  Go on.

Adam Everyone just stands by and watches while this really hot guy fucks me. So I decide to put on a show for them.

Toby How?

Adam I moan, I arch my back.

Toby God, I can only imagine what that looked like.

Adam Can you?

Toby I'm picturing it right now.

Adam How's it look?

Toby Really fucking good.

Adam Eventually another guy wants to take a turn.

Toby Did you let him?

Adam Yeah. So now this other guy and I are fucking. Then another guy takes a turn, then another. Eventually I lose count.

Toby Jesus, Adam.

Adam Meanwhile, everyone is touching me. Thirty hands, fifteen mouths on my body. It wasn't even me in that moment, it was this other version of me. I remember thinking to myself: 'This is how it feels to truly be alive.'
    I start to get close. I stand up on a bench. By now I'm completely covered in sweat and lube and spit. I start to jack myself off, bringing myself closer and closer to orgasm. All eyes are on me. Wanting me, encouraging me, demanding of me that I cum for them. And then finally, standing over them, my world contracts into a tight little ball and I release myself . . . I spray my cum all over them, like I'm anointing them. I've never cum so hard or so much in all my life. It was the closest I've ever been to genuine ecstasy.

Toby reaches for Adam. Adam allows Toby to touch him.

One by one, everyone starts to cum. It was beautiful to watch. I was euphoric. I remember thinking: I always want to feel like I do right now. This moment, this feeling, I want to live in this moment for the rest of my life.

Toby continues to feel Adam.

Slowly my euphoria started to fade and a thought starts to form, like Adam Lucas McDowell returning to this hot, sweaty body: none of those guys had been wearing condoms. And suddenly, I'm awoken from my dream to the realization that I'd just barebacked with at least a dozen guys.

Adam moves away from Toby.

I got down off the bench and made my way out of the stall. Everyone was grabbing at me, wanting me to stay. Suddenly their touches felt like violations. I ran to the locker room and quickly dressed. I left with my clothes sticking to my body, still sweaty and covered in lube and spit and cum. I smelled so disgustingly. I ran to my hotel. When I got to my room, I took the hottest shower I could stand. I cleaned myself and discovered I was bleeding. I could see it going down the drain. I got out of the shower and looked at my clothes. There was blood all over my underwear and inside my jeans.

Toby What did you do?

Adam I called my mother, telling her it was just one guy. She called a friend of hers, a surgeon at Sloan-Kettering. This surgeon called a friend of his in Prague, who wrote me a prescription for PEP. I flew home the next day and we went up to Vermont for Christmas. I got really sick on Christmas Day. It felt like the worst flu ever. My mother took me to the hospital where I got a rapid HIV test. It came back inconclusive. The doctor ordered blood work. But it was Christmas and I had to wait three days for the lab to re-open. Worst Christmas of my life. Three days later, my mom and I drove back to the hospital for the results. They found the virus in my blood. Trace amounts. Barely detectable. But still detectable. HIV positive.

Toby I had no idea.

Adam The doctor told me to keep taking the PEP treatment for the rest of the month. I went back to school and tried to distract myself with work. I would lay awake at night obsessively going over that night in my mind. Which one gave this to me? How could an experience that transcendent yield consequences so terrifying? Once the month was out, I went to the health center on campus. They did another round of tests. This time they came back negative across the board.

Toby Oh. So . . . what does that mean?

Adam It means I was exposed to the virus, I became temporarily HIV positive and the PEP treatment worked. It means I came as close to the edge as possible and at the last second I was rescued. Kinda like what my parents did for me when I was two weeks old.

Silence.

Don't ever tell me that I don't know what it's like to be scared to death.

Toby Adam, I –

Adam It's getting late.

Toby Adam, I –

Adam I should get to bed.

Toby Adam –

Adam Night, Toby.

Toby I'll, um, I'll see you tomorrow.

Morgan That night, Adam McDowell learned an important lesson. He had power. Far more than he ever imagined.

Young Man 1 He wondered what else he might be capable of.

End of Scene One.

SCENE TWO

October 9, 2016. Eric's Thirty-Fourth Birthday

Morgan Eric awoke on his thirty-fourth birthday to an email from the Glass family's attorney. In exchange for a settlement, the Glass family had agreed to vacate the property at midnight on January 1, 2017. Eric busied himself with preparations for his birthday brunch, pushing thoughts of the future to the back of his mind.

Eric His friends arrived at eleven.

1. Eric and Toby's Apartment

Eric, Walter, Tristan, Jasper, Jason 1 and Jason 2. Jason 2 is showing Walter pictures of their wedding.

Jason 2 And that's us in the garden before the ceremony.

Walter Lovely.

Jason 2 And that's us still in the garden before the ceremony.

Walter Very nice.

Jason 2 And that's us in the garden before the ceremony but from a different angle.

Walter Yes, I see that.

Jasper Your partner is Henry Wilcox, right? The real estate developer.

Walter Yes, that's right.

Jason 1 How long have you been together?

Walter Almost thirty-six years.

Jason 2 Wow!

Jason 1 Have you ever thought of getting married?

Walter No.

Jason 2 Why not?

Walter Never saw the need.

Jason 2 Yeah, but the party. And the gift registry.

Jason 1 What happens if he dies before you? Do you ever worry about that?

Walter No.

Jason 2 Oh, this is one of my favorites. Look.

Walter Still in the garden, are we?

Jason 2 It's such a lovely garden.

Tristan What do you do for a living, Walter?

Walter Fortunately, I've never needed to work. I raised Henry's sons for him, which was work enough.

Jason 1 You and your partner have children?

Walter Henry has two boys from his marriage. Their mother died when they were young.

Eric Really, Walter? I didn't know that.

Jason 2 Ooh, did you adopt them?

Walter No, but I raised them.

Jason 2 Well, speaking of adopting . . . (*To Jason 1.*) Should we tell them?

Jason 1 I think you just did.

Jason 2 Jason and I are adopting a baby in the new year!

The Lads react excitedly.

Jason 1 It's still not completely certain.

Jason 2 But we found a mother.

Jason 1 She lives in Denver.

Jason 2 She's due early January.

Eric God, you guys are gonna be parents.

Jason 1 If everything works out.

Walter Do all of you plan to have children?

Jason 1 ⎫ Obviously we do.

Jason 2 ⎬ We're gonna have three!

Tristan ⎭ I'd like to some day.

Jasper No fucking way.

Walter Why not for you, Jasper?

Jasper Children are dirty, diseased bloodsuckers who get their grubby little fingers all over your expensive furniture. Children drain you of your vitality. Children rob you of your sleep. Children age you prematurely and then have the nerve to resent you for it on their therapist's couch, which you have to pay for. So start saving now.

Walter Well, as long as you've given it some thought.

Jasper If I ever do find the person I'm meant to be with, I wanna fuck him senseless every day. Go mountain climbing. Have an orgy in the Pines. Fist a twink together.

Jason 2 Well *he's* not babysitting.

Jasper Yes I am!

Eric Let's eat!

Young Man 4 The brunch commenced and Walter withdrew into silence.

81

Walter lights a cigarette. Stunned silence from Eric and the Lads. Walter notices.

Walter Do you mind if I smoke?

They all clearly do, but:

Eric I don't mind. (*To the rest.*) Do you?

Tristan I don't mind.

Jasper I don't mind.

Jason 2 I'm expecting a child.

Then:

I don't mind.

Young Man 3 Eric was afraid Walter wasn't enjoying himself nearly as much as he was enjoying his cigarette.

Young Man 4 And so he attempted to bring the subject around to a topic about which he was certain Walter would have some insight.

Eric You know what I miss? I miss the feeling that being gay was like being a member of a secret club.

Jason 2 You mean being in the closet?

Eric No, I mean that liminal state when we were out but also, I don't know, still kinda mysterious and opaque to society.

Tristan Oh, like: friends were welcome to visit our little club but only members were allowed to access the full benefits.

Eric Yes! And in order to fully join, you needed people to help bring you in.

Jason 2 You've just described Soho House.

Eric No, I'm describing a community. Everything was a little secretive, you know?

Tristan But not in a shameful way.

Eric No.

Tristan More like in a 'this is our thing' kinda way.

Eric Yes! It was a secret culture with a secret language and shared, secret experiences.

Tristan That really was the best part of being gay, wasn't it?

Jasper I always thought the best part was the orgasms.

Jason 2 Being gay doesn't feel remarkable anymore. It's like, 'Oh you're gay? Ho-hum, what other tricks can you do?'

Jasper But the point of all that work at visibility was to not feel stigmatized. To not have our sexual identities be our primary identities.

Jason 2 I never felt stigmatized, I felt *special*! I *like* being gay.

Jason 1 But being gay isn't all you are, baby. You're a teacher, you're married, you're about to become one goddamn sexy father.

Eric I think my question is: what does it mean now to be a gay man?

Tristan There are as many answers to that question as they are gay men to ask it.

Eric Yes, of course. But there were also several clearly identifiable cultural markers.

Jason 2 Are you talking about drag queens and camp and being Friends of Dorothy?

Eric Yes, in part.

Jason 2 About seeing every revival of *Gypsy* since at least Tyne Daly?

Jasper But that's just a clichéd part of the gay identity.

Eric I just mean there are certain identifiable, broadly applicable cultural markers that are specific to the gay community that I fear we are starting to lose.

Tristan For example?

Eric For example . . .

Jason 2 Sing out, Louise!

Eric Um . . . well, take camp, for instance.

Jasper Ugh, I am so over camp.

Jason 2 How can anyone be over camp?

Jasper It's like nails on a chalkboard to me at this point.

Eric What's your idea of camp, Jasper?

Jasper You know – Liza Minnelli.

Jason 1 Liza's not camp. Liza's a diva.

Jason 2 But Liza singing 'Copacabana' in a nightclub with the Muppets?

Tristan *and* **Jason 2** That's camp.

Eric Exactly!

Tristan See? That's the problem. Camp has been watered down to the point that most people can't even define it.

Jason 1 Camp is about recognizing the ridiculousness of life, of our society –

Jason 2 – of ourselves.

Tristan It's the weapon of the powerless to puncture the pretenses of the powerful.

Jasper Yeah, but now that Obama is president –
   Now that the historically powerless have taken the reins of power for themselves, haven't we effectively moved on from that need?

Tristan Ask any mother of a black child in America that question.

Eric There will always be powerless people in the world.

Jason 1 And powerful people to mock.

Tristan Which means that camp, unlike disco, will never die.

Jason 2 Which is good, because I looove me some camp, baby!

Jasper Yeah, Jason, we know.

Jason 2 Because I am a big fucking nelly faggot queen and I do not care who knows it.

Jasper Yasss kween!

Tristan Oh! That is what really drives me crazy: this whole 'yasss kween' thing. My fourteen-year-old niece said 'yass kween' at Thanksgiving last year and I was like, 'Who the fuck have you been hanging out with?' and she was all like –

Young Man 4 'Oh Uncle Tristan, that's from *Broad City*.'

Tristan And I was like, 'The hell it is. That phrase has been toppling out of the painted lips of drag queens since before you were born.' They have appropriated a phrase from drag culture – much of which was itself appropriated from ball culture – and they've built a brand off it. Every time I hear a straight girl say 'yassss kween,' I wanna say to them, 'Tell me who Willi Ninja is and then you can play.'

Jasper But we can't on the one hand insist on more representation in popular culture and then cry foul when our culture starts to get disseminated into the culture at large.

Jason 1 Only if that kind of cultural visibility also comes with the kind of societal participation that matters.

Jasper Such as . . .?

Jason 1 Such as . . .

Jason 2 Come on baby you got this.

Jason 1 Okay. Harvey Milk!

Lads react loudly.

Tristan Oh God, Jason just played the Harvey Milk card!

Jason 1 I mean, sure it's great Sean Penn won an Oscar for playing Harvey Milk, but American students are still taught nothing about queer history. Tristan's niece may know 'yass kween' but I bet she can tell you nothing about the UpStairs Lounge fire, Barbara Gittings, or the sip-in at Julius'.

Tristan And I'm still waiting on that Bayard Rustin biopic nobody's yet bothered to make.

Eric Yes, my point exactly! It feels like all the different facets of queer culture are being stripped for parts and that the community that I came up in is slowly fading away.

Jason 1 Some things are definitely changing for the better, though, right? Marriage equality being the obvious example.

Jasper Oh, and also Truvada. *That's* definitely a game-changer.

Tristan For those who can afford it.

Eric How has Truvada changed things for you, Tristan?

Tristan Used to be, disclosing my status to a partner would lead to either one of two results: the stigma of rejection or sometimes the intimacy of understanding. Truvada has changed that. There's far less stigma now but I also feel like I've lost some of that intimacy. Now it's sort of like, 'Oh, you're poz? Ho-hum, fuck me, daddy.' Not that I'm complaining. Nor are they, for that matter. But that was inconceivable to me when I sero-converted eleven years ago.

Eric Has it really been eleven years, Tristan?

Tristan And I am healthier today than ever before. I've got so many extra T-cells I could start selling them on eBay.

Eric You know what I just realized? I miss gay bars.

Tristan Me too.

Jason 2 Dancing at Escuelita.

Jasper Wonder Bar.

Tristan Roxy.

Jason 1 Twilo.

Tristan No Parking.

Jason 2 Musical Mondays at Splash.

Eric Gay bars used to be safe spaces for people like us to be ourselves and to find others like us. Now everyone just goes onto Grindr. But what about a twenty-year-old kid who's not looking for sex, but rather for community, for

87

a connection with something that helps him understand himself? Or the sixty-year-old man who's looking for the same?

Jasper Or the sixty-year-old who's looking for the twenty-year-old?

Tristan, Jason 1, Jason 2 That's gonna be you.

Eric What happens to that shared culture? If being gay only describes who we love and who we fuck but not also how we encounter the world, then gay culture and gay community will start to disappear. And we still need that community. Because this country is still filled with people who hate us with vengeful, murderous fanaticism.

Jason 1 I'm sorry. 'Vengeful, murderous fanaticism'? I think you may be going a little overboard.

Eric You don't think that's accurate?

Jason 1 I don't think it takes into account all the progress we've made in the last several years. I mean, look at where we are now. Progress has *happened*.

Tristan Tell that to the kids at Pulse.

Jason 1 I know. I don't mean to minimize that.

Tristan But . . .

Jason 1 No, my point is that there will always be vengeful, murderous fanatics in the world. That will never change. What can change, what has changed and what must continue to change is the way our society *protects* people from vengeful, murderous fanatics. I mean, let's be honest, I think we can all stipulate that, barring an unforeseen tragedy, we in this room are a lot less vulnerable than others in our community. Now we have a chance to build on the progress that has been made in the last eight years. How do the people in this room – who have largely benefited from the Obama

88

years – continue to fight for our community? What happens now?

Jasper Let's talk about our responsibilities to our trans siblings.

Jason 2 Let's talk about growing rates of poverty within our community.

Tristan Let's talk about the resurgence of HIV among gay men of color.

Eric Let's talk about the rising rates of addiction, suicide and homelessness among LGBT youth.

Jason 1 Yes! These are the things that will require just as much of our blood, sweat and tears as marriage equality did. And these are the things we have the chance to make some real progress on once Clinton is elected.

Walter Are we that certain she's going to win?

The Lads seem sure.

What happens if you're wrong?

Jasper It's the Senate we should be focused on, anyway.

Tristan There's no way she's not gonna win.

Jason 2 Read the polls!

Jason 1 Nate Silver is never wrong.

Eric I think what Walter means to say is that we should never assume anything – right, Walter?

Walter In part. I'm also afraid she's going to lose.

Silence.

I'm sorry. It's Eric's birthday. And we're all having such a / nice time.

Eric No, it's probably worth thinking about: what if the unthinkable happens?

Tristan ⎤	My girl's gonna win!
Jason 2 ⎪	It's gonna be a blowout.
Jasper ⎬	We're gonna take Arizona this year.
Jason 1 ⎦	I set my watch by Nate Silver's predictions.

Eric But what if it does? We need our community, we need our history. How else can we teach the next generation who they are and how they got here? Human culture from time immemorial has been transmitted through stories. Think about the ancient epics: the *Odyssey*, the *Mahabharata*, oral histories that allowed cultures to understand themselves. In order to become an honorable Greek, one had to study the actions of Odysseus. A young Hindu would reflect on the conversation between Arjuna and Krishna on the battlefield. My grandmother, from as early as I can remember, taught me about the Shoah and her experiences as a refugee. And perhaps as a result of these intergenerational conversations, passed along in some cases for millennia, history is conveyed and cultures survived. Greeks thump their chests and reflect on the invasion of Troy. Black children stand just a little taller at the mention of Rosa Parks. And in queer culture, we feel the stirring of pride when we reflect on the meaning of Stonewall, Marsha Johnson, Sylvia Rivera, Edie Windsor, Matthew Shepard, Islan Nettles, and the bravery of the people on the front lines of the epidemic. And to let that go means we've relinquished a part of ourselves. If we can't have a conversation with our past, then what will be our future? Who are we? And more importantly: who will we become?

Morgan And then, Eric thought but did not say:

Eric Who will *I* become?

2. *Hallway*

Walter It has been years since I've been in a room with younger gay men. You all give me such hope. And I found what you in particular had to say was incredibly thoughtful and moving.

Eric Just the after-effects of three glasses of wine.

Walter It felt more like a *cri de coeur*.

Eric Just grandstanding to show off my education.

Walter Don't, Eric. Do not discount my words the way you discount yourself.

Eric I wasn't trying / to dis —

Walter I admire you tremendously. I see in you a version of myself I had long since forgotten.

Eric Walter – I don't know what to say to that.

Walter When I don't know what to say I find it's best to say nothing.

Eric That honestly has never occurred to me. I can't tell you what your friendship has meant to me this autumn.

Walter does not answer – lost, it seems, in reverie.

Walter?

Walter I would very much like to show you to my house upstate.

Eric Yes, I would love that. We should take a trip sometime.

Walter How about tonight?

Eric Tonight?

Walter Yes. Right now. The cherry tree should be in full reds and oranges. It'll do us both good.

Eric I would love to see it.

Walter Wonderful.

Eric It's just that tonight's not . . . tonight's not the –

He then seems to have a change of heart.

Yes. I would love to see your house tonight.

Walter There's a train a seven-thirty. If we hurry we can make it.

Charles and Paul Wilcox enter.

Charles You're gonna get a ticket, Paul.

Paul The hydrant was ten feet away.

Charles Still gonna get a ticket.

Paul It's a $50 parking spot.

Charles Hey there he is!

Walter Charlie? Paul? What are you doing here?

Charles We're taking you to dinner.

Paul Charles wanted to surprise you.

Walter Eric, these are Henry's sons I was telling you about, Charles and Paul Wilcox.

Eric It's so nice to meet you. / I've heard so much about you.

Charles What are you doing in the hallway?

Paul Are you locked out?

Walter No, we were just leaving to go up to my house.

Paul I'll call a locksmith.

Paul takes out his phone, dials.

Charles What, upstate? No, it's way too late. We're taking you to dinner.

Paul (*into his phone*) Susie, get me a locksmith. Walter's locked out of the apartment again.

Walter No, Paul, I'm not locked out –

Charles I booked your favorite table at La Grenouille.

Paul (*to Susie, on phone*) There might be a spare in Pop's office.

Walter I promised Eric I'd show him the house.

Charles You're not going to say no to us, are you? We haven't seen you in weeks.

Walter (*to Eric*) I'm so sorry – I didn't know they were coming.

Eric It's fine. We can go another time.

Paul (*to Susie, on phone*) What do you mean, 'What do they look like?' They're keys. They look like keys.

Walter Eric, you should come with us. It's his birthday today.

Eric Oh, no. I don't want to intrude.

Walter It won't be any intrusion.

Charles He doesn't want to intrude. Come on, Walter. Paul parked in front of a hydrant.

Paul (*to Charles*) That hydrant was twenty feet away. (*To Susie, on phone.*) Call me back if you find them. (*To Charles.*) She can't find the keys. (*To Eric.*) Who the fuck are you?

Walter Eric, are you sure you don't want to join us?

Eric It wasn't meant to for us to go tonight.

Walter I'm so sorry. Thank you for understanding.

Charles Walter, let's go.

Paul Who the fuck is that guy?

Walter I won't forget my promise to you.

Walter, Charles and Paul exit.

End of Scene Two.

SCENE THREE

Autumn 2016

Young Man 1 But it seemed that Walter *had* forgotten his promise. In the weeks following Eric's birthday, Eric saw little of Walter. He was rarely home whenever Eric visited and, whenever Eric did catch him in, Walter was never in the mood for more than a cursory exchange of pleasantries.

Toby Eric flew to Chicago to attend the opening of Toby's play.

1. 'Loved Boy' Opens

Morgan The play received ecstatic reviews.

Young Man 7 The director Tom Durrell's staging was deemed revelatory.

Young Man 1 Adam's performance was hailed as one of the most thrilling stage debuts that anyone could remember.

Young Man 5 It was said in those weeks that the most dangerous place to be was in between Adam –

Young Man 3 – and any agent hoping to sign him.

Young Man 1 The production was a hit.

Young Man 2 Offers were made and plans were hatched for a Broadway transfer the following summer.

Toby Toby was hailed as the premiere writer of his generation. His talents were breathlessly compared to Salinger, Albee, Eugene O'-fucking-Neill.

Morgan No.

Toby Why not?

Morgan Because then what?

Toby Then? He lives happily ever after.

Morgan No, the response to Toby's writing was decidedly less effusive than that.

Toby How much less?

Young Man 1 His talent was recognized but the achievement was not considered as great as his colleagues'.

Morgan The impression one got was that Toby Darling had crafted the perfect vehicle for Tom Durrell and Adam McDowell to prove their genius.

Toby That's bullshit.

Morgan And yet, that is what happened.

Toby They didn't say one positive thing about the writing? Nothing to indicate that Toby deserved any credit for this success? After all that work? After all these years?

Young Man 1 Not in the way that Toby needed to hear.

Toby Well fuck that. Toby flies to Los Angeles where, over the course of three dizzying weeks, he drops his longtime agent for a new team at a high-powered agency, he takes on a manager, lawyers up, and promptly sells the film rights to *Loved Boy*. (*To Morgan.*) *That's* what Toby does.

Young Man 8 Wouldn't Toby have made a lot more money if he waited until *after* it opened on Broadway to sell the film rights?

All eyes on Toby. Then:

Toby Fuck!

2. *November 8, 2016*

Eric On election night, Eric gathered with his friends to watch the returns –

Young Man 5 – while Toby had dinner with his new agents at Mr Chow's in Beverly Hills.

Young Man 6 Eric bought noisemakers and small American flags for the occasion.

Young Man 7 But from as early as seven o'clock, it was clear to Jasper that something was off.

Jasper Eric, I'm worried about Florida.

Eric Really?

Jasper Pinellas County is practically a dead heat right now. That shouldn't be happening.

Eric It's early yet, Jasper.

Jasper A Democrat should be leading by double digits in St Pete right out of the gate. And fuck, she's behind in Hillsboro County.

Morgan Eric texted Toby:

Eric Are you watching? Call me.

Jasper I'm telling you guys, this is not looking good.

Jason 1 Nate Silver still has her at 86 per cent.

Jason 2 She just won Connecticut!

Eric Oh, and Massachusetts!

Morgan Nine o'clock:

Tristan Clinton takes New York!

Jasper Arizona, Colorado, Michigan, Minnesota, New Mexico, Wisconsin: all too close to call.

Morgan Ten o'clock . . .

Jasper Nevada too close to call. Utah too close to call.

Morgan And then at 10:21 . . .

Jasper Oh fuck, they just called Ohio.

Jason 1 Nate Silver has her at 72 per cent.

Morgan 11:07 . . .

Jasper They just called North Carolina.

Jason 1 Sixty-seven per cent.

Morgan And 11:30 . . .

Jasper Fuck, there goes Florida.

Jason 1 Fifty-three per cent.

Morgan Eric texted Toby:

Eric Where are you? This is bad. Is this really happening?

Morgan For hours, they watched with growing dread as state after state was called.

Jasper We still have a firewall in the rust belt. And Arizona might still be in play.

Morgan And then, nothing. Three hours of waiting as

precinct after precinct slowly started to report. The Jasons went home. Tristan fell asleep in the guest room. Eric and Jasper finished another bottle of wine as they waited, waited for a miracle. And then at 3:04 in the morning . . .

Jasper They just called Pennsylvania. That's it, then. It's over.

Eric It's over.

Morgan A week later, Toby returned from Los Angeles.

3. Eric and Toby's Apartment

Toby You've known for a year we were losing the apartment and you didn't tell me?

Eric I've known it was a possibility.

Toby Why didn't you say anything / to me?

Eric I didn't want to worry you.

Toby Don't treat me like a child, Eric.

Eric I'm not, Toby / I simply . . .

Toby The night we got engaged, I mentioned having the wedding here at the apartment and you said 'Mmhmm, yeah, maybe.' Did you know then?

Eric Yes.

Toby How long had you known?

Eric Only a couple of hours.

Toby You proposed to me the day you found out we were being evicted?

Eric The day I found out it was a possibility.

Toby You see how that looks, right?

Eric No . . .

Toby It looks like entrapment.

Eric How did I entrap you?

Toby By luring me into a marriage under false pretenses.

Eric Are you saying that if you *had* known about the apartment, you might have made a different decision?

Toby I'm saying that I didn't have all the information I needed when you asked me to marry you.

Eric What other information did you need? Are you with me because of this apartment?

Toby Of course not!

Eric So then why should it matter?

Toby Because you weren't honest with me.

Eric I'm being honest with you now. We're going to have to move at the end of the year. I'm sorry I didn't say anything. I truly didn't want to worry you needlessly. But, with your advances on the play, I figure we'll have enough money for a down payment on a small apartment. And maybe if there's any left over we could start saving up to adopt a baby – in a year or two. Oh Toby, come on! Everything's going to be fine. At least now that you're back, we can finally start planning for the future.

Toby I can't just start looking at apartments with you, Eric. I can't just sit down and make plans for the future.

Eric Why not?

Toby Because who the fuck knows what's going to happen between now and then? And in the meantime,

I've got a lot of work to do. My play is coming to Broadway.
   I just can't make a commitment like that right now.

Eric Please, Toby, just tell me what the fuck is going on?

Toby I don't want to get married. Okay? I don't want to get married.

Eric Right now?
   At all?
   Or to me?
   Toby? Toby please answer me.

Toby I don't know.

Eric Yes, you do.

Toby I don't want to marry you.

Eric Why not?

Toby I just . . . I just feel we're in different places right now.

Eric What does that even mean, Toby?

Toby I don't –

Eric I have done nothing but love and support you. I have walked beside you for seven years. Now that I don't have this apartment to offer you / now that success is in your grasp, you don't need me anymore.

Toby It has nothing to do with your apartment!

Eric Maybe you even think you can do better. At least be honest and tell me that, Toby.

Toby I just want something different.

Eric Did you fuck Adam in Chicago?

Toby No!

Eric Do you want to fuck Adam?

Toby Yes! Of course I want to fuck Adam, who doesn't?

Eric I don't.

Toby Then there is something seriously wrong with you, Eric. He's gorgeous.

Eric There's more to people than beauty.

Toby You would have to tell yourself that, wouldn't you?
    I did not mean that.

Eric Actually, that's the first honest thing you've said this entire conversation. And since we're finally telling each other the truth, you should know that I hated your fucking play.

Toby Wow, Eric. I never thought you would stoop so low as to lash out like that. That play is the greatest thing I've ever done in my life. We're a huge fucking hit and we're moving to Broadway.

Eric Because of Tom's production and Adam's performance.

Toby Oh fuck you, Eric. I worked my ass off on that play. I have been rolling that boulder up the hill for the last decade of my life.

Eric Who stood by your side while you were rolling your fucking boulder up the hill? You had the luxury of struggling for seven years because of me / and what I gave you.

Toby That is bullshit, Eric.
    What you 'gave' me? You didn't give me anything. I built my life from the ground up. God, I am so sick of your holier-than-thou, thoughtful, sweet and kind fucking bullshit. You act like you're above the fray, can't be touched, fucking Yale, fucking Fieldston, fucking save

the world by strongly worded Facebook post, when secretly you're just as manipulative and as self-involved and as frightened as the rest of us. But you slap on this veneer of middle-class perfection and you think that protects you from having to be a real person. But real people are ugly, Eric. Real people are compromised. Real people disappoint each other. Because the world is ugly and compromised and disappointing. And I'm sorry I can't be perfect like you. I was never given that option. I have no choice but to be a real person.

Eric That is the last thing that you are, Toby. You've become so good at spinning people / you think you can spin me, too.

Toby I don't 'spin' anyone.

Eric But I know that your book was a fraud from start to finish / and your play was –

Toby Fraud?! Fuck you, Eric.

Eric And your play was even worse. Not without talent, but worse: without truth. Toby, you are so afraid of actually being known – of really looking at yourself – that you have spent the last decade of your life constructing this elaborate narrative that has nothing to do with the truth. What happened to you as a child was unconscionable / and it hurts me every single day to know that it did.

Toby Don't you fucking dare / use that against me.

Eric But that was not the great tragedy of your life, Toby. No, the great tragedy of your life was denying that it *was* your life, and insisting on another at the expense of the truth. I couldn't even look at you after I saw your play. Because it was a betrayal of the frightened little boy you once were. And soon all of New York is going to see it and I will be the only one who'll remember who you really are. And that's why you want to get as far away from me as possible: because I would remind you every day of what a fraud you are and what wasted potential your life has become. And that's what you're too much of a coward to say.

Silence.

Toby Well, Eric. If there's anyone who knows anything about wasted potential, it is you. And if you feel this way about me – if this is who you think I really am – then why the fuck did you stay with me for seven years?

Eric Because I love you, you fucking piece of shit!

Henry Wilcox enters.

Henry Am I interrupting something?

Eric } No.
Toby } Yes.

Eric Henry. Is everything all right?

Henry I wanted to come by to let you know . . . Walter's . . . Walter's gone.

Eric Gone?

Henry He died this morning.
    Charles took him to the hospital yesterday. I flew back just in time to . . .
    I know how close you and he had become while I was away.

Eric Henry, I don't even know what to say. I'm so sorry. Do you want to / come in?

Henry No, I . . . no. Thank you. I thought you'd want to know.

Eric Henry, I –

Henry exits.

Toby Eric.

Eric No.

Toby Eric, I'm sorry.

Eric You've ruined everything, Toby. Everything you touch, you ruin.

End of Scene Three.

SCENE FOUR

Autumn 2016

1. Henry and Walter's Apartment

Morgan Walter had been cremated, per his lifelong understanding with Henry. The doctors told of a body eaten entirely away by cancer. Walter had told no one of his illness. Not even Henry. Henry had already buried his parents, one sibling, the mother of his sons and friends far too numerous to count. But true mourning had largely eluded him. With Walter's passing, he could avoid it no longer. After thirty-six years together, Walter was gone. Henry's sons gathered at his apartment every evening.

Henry You don't have to come by every night.

Paul We were just in the neighborhood.

Charles Were you taking a nap?

Henry Yeah.

Charles Were you able to sleep?

Henry A little.

Charles Should I make some coffee?

Paul Maybe a scotch?

Henry I'm fine, thank you.

Paul Everyone's been asking about you at the office.

Henry Shit. Are things falling apart already?

Paul No, that's not what I –

Charles Everyone just misses you, Pop.

Henry I should probably go in tomorrow, show my face.

Charles ⎫ There's no rush.
Paul ⎭ You don't have to do that.

Henry No, I'm done stewing. Walter wouldn't approve.

Charles No, it's true. He wouldn't.

Paul No.

Charles No.

Paul No.

Charles Paul.

Henry What?

Charles A package arrived for you today. From a woman in Queens.

Paul She says she was Walter's nurse at the hospital.

Charles Inside was an envelope, with your name on it, in Walter's handwriting.

Morgan A chill trickled down Henry's spine. This was the closest these men had ever come to a spiritual communion with the dead.

>   *Charles hands over Walter's letter. Henry opens it. It is as if he has seen a ghost.*

Charles Pop, are you okay?

Paul What does it say?

Walter 'To Henry –
   I should like Eric Glass to have my house.'

Charles *and* **Paul** That's it?

Henry That's it.

Paul Who the fuck is Eric Glass?

Henry He was a friend of Walter's. He and his partner live a few floors up. Apparently the two of them had spent a lot of time together while I was away.

Paul What do you mean, 'spent time'?

Henry I just mean that Eric had been kind to Walter.

Charles Kind enough for Walter to leave him his house?

Paul This is bullshit – lemme see that. (*Grabbing it from Charles.*) But it's written in pencil. Pencil doesn't count.

Charles There's no date, it isn't witnessed.

Paul There's not even a signature.

Henry It's Walter's handwriting.

Charles It's not a legal document, Pop.

Henry It's his last request.

Charles Why would he leave that house to a total stranger? He loved that house.

Paul Hey – I bet this Glass guy tricked Walter into writing that.

Charles Yes! He probably knew that Walter was sick.

Paul Have you checked Walter's bank account lately?

Charles He might have cleared him out already.

Paul The fucker. We should call the cops.

Charles Yes!

Henry All right, both of you, that's enough.

Charles Come on, Pop. Don't you think this is just a little suspicious?

Henry Walter was always giving away books and knick-knacks to people.

Paul But never an entire house!

Charles He was on so much morphine at the end.

Paul That fucking nurse should be fired for it.

Henry If Eric had needed somewhere to live, I could understand it. And even if he did, he wouldn't want to live up there.

Paul It's three hours from the city. We don't even go there anymore.

Charles That's not the point, Paul. That house is a part of our family. It's where we spent the summer after Mom died. That house meant everything to Walter. He couldn't have meant to give it to a stranger.

Paul So then what do we do?

Charles looks at his father for a tacit go-ahead and then pulls out a lighter and sets the letter ablaze.

Morgan Refrain, if you can, from judging the Wilcoxes too harshly. Should they have offered their home to Eric? Logic – and even emotion – suggests not. What they could not have known was that to Walter it had been more than a house: it had been a spiritual possession, for which he sought a spiritual heir. No; the Wilcox men are not to be blamed for their decision.
   Except.
   One hard fact remains. They did neglect a personal

appeal. The man who had died did say to them, 'Do this,' and they answered: 'We will not.'

End of Act Two.

Act Three

SCENE ONE

1. Adam's Apartment

Toby on Adam's doorstep, soaking wet.

Toby Is this a bad time?

Adam You're soaked.

Toby Oh. Yeah.

Adam Let me get you a towel.

Toby That's okay.

Adam You're dripping on the rug.

Toby Sorry for barging in on you like this.

Adam It's fine. What's going on?

Toby Eric and I broke up tonight.

Adam *Wait*, what?! How? / What happened?

Toby I could really use a drink right now.

Adam Um, sure. Do you want some wine / or –

Toby Wine's a nice girl but she's no match for tonight. I need whiskey. Lots of it. And bring me something while I wait for it.

Adam Oh, Toby.

He pours Toby a drink.

Toby 'Oh Toby.' I'm going to have that phrase *emblazoned* on my tombstone.

Adam What happened?

Toby Eric and I had the Hiroshima of fights.

Adam What about?

Toby You.

Morgan But what Toby actually said was:

Toby The thing is I can't even remember. All I know is that I told him I didn't want to get married.

Adam Oh, Toby.

Toby There it is again. This time with judgment attached.

Adam Not judgment . . . bewilderment. You're Eric and Toby.

Toby Toby and Eric.
He fucking kicked me out, can you believe it? Jesus, I'm homeless.

Adam Do you still love Eric?

Toby I don't know anything right now. I think I might be a monster.

Adam Go home. Talk to him.

Toby God, no. I'm sure he's summoned the coven by now. They're probably gathered in the apartment doing incantations against me. I'll probably get a hotel.

Adam I mean, you can stay here if you want. My parents are in Vermont.

Toby Yeah, okay. I'm sorry to drop all this on you.

Adam It's what friends do, right?

Toby Like I fuckin' know.

Adam And in the morning you'll call him and you'll work this out.

Toby The thing is, Adam, I don't want to work it out.

Adam What do you want, then, Toby?

Toby You.

Morgan But what Toby actually said was:

Toby I don't know anymore. I'm sorry I haven't been in touch since you got back from Chicago. Things have been nuts lately. Hey, I sold the film rights.

Adam Oh, good for you, Toby!

Toby Yeah. Good for good ol' Toby.

Adam Wait, you sold the film rights *before* Broadway? Wouldn't you have made more / money if you'd –

Toby Just shut up, Adam. Hit me again.

Adam I got the offer for Broadway yesterday.

Toby Hey, that's great! I'm glad that all worked out.

Adam What do you mean, 'worked out'?

Toby That they ended up going with you, after all.

Adam Why wouldn't they?

Toby What? Oh. There was talk of replacing you but that idea went nowhere.

Adam Who wanted to replace me?

Toby No one, just the producers. Don't worry, you're fine. I insisted that they keep you. Glad to hear they made the offer.

Adam Which of the producers wanted to replace me?

Toby Oh God, I shouldn't have said anything. There was the briefest talk of finding a star but that fizzled very quickly.

Adam Tom told me everyone was excited for me to do the show in New York. Tom said I was the star.

Toby You talked to Tom recently?

Adam Oh. Well . . .

Toby What?

Adam Well . . . I've been meaning to tell you, actually. Tom and I are . . . we're kinda dating.

Toby You and . . . Tom?

Adam Yeah.

Toby He's fifty years old.

Adam He's forty-seven. I wanted to tell you but you've been so busy. It started just after we opened. I didn't think that he – anyway, it took us both by surprise.

Toby starts to implode.

Toby, are you okay? Toby?

Toby You're fucking Tom Durrell?

Adam Toby –

Toby You're fucking the director of my play?

Adam He's my director, too.

Toby Which is why you shouldn't be fucking him!

Adam I mean, it's more than just sex. We . . . we kinda fell in love.

Toby Oh, I don't believe this. You're in love with Tom Durrell?

Adam I think I might be. He's taking me to Brazil for Christmas.

Toby I don't even know what to say to you right now.

Adam You could try being happy for me.

Toby Yeah, but Tom fucking Durrell, Adam?

Adam What's wrong with Tom?

Toby What's wrong with *me*?

Adam Toby?

Toby tries to kiss Adam. Adam pulls away.

Toby.

Toby grabs him and pulls him toward him. Adam resists.

Toby, stop.

Toby pulls him back once more into a kiss.

Toby, stop! Why did you do that?

Toby Because I love you.

Adam No you don't.

Toby I love you.

Adam Stop saying that.

Toby I ended things with Eric because of you.

Adam No, that isn't true.

Toby Yes, it is! I came here tonight to tell you that.

Adam No you didn't. That's not why you came here.

Toby Please, you have to believe me. My heart was pure. My heart is always pure. Unfortunately it happens to be surrounded by the rest of me.

Adam You're upset and-and-and you're confused –

Toby I love you.

Adam And you're drunk.

Toby I've been in love with you since that night I walked you home in the rain.

Adam Toby, we're friends. Eric is like my brother.

Toby That's what's made all of this so agonizing. I fell in love with you and I kept falling in love with you and now I'm completely, irreparably, disastrously in love with you. You have to know that, Adam. I think that maybe you feel the same.

Adam No, I don't.

Toby Don't feel like you have to be in any rush to answer.

Adam I don't feel the same as you. I don't love you, Toby. In fact, I want you to leave.

Toby I'm sorry, Adam. I promise this is not how I wanted this to go.

Morgan How *did* you want this to go?

Toby Well, obviously better than this!

Adam Just leave.

Toby Please don't go to South America with Tom.

Adam That is none of your business.

Toby Please don't choose him over me.

Adam This isn't about you, Toby.

Toby Yes it is, because I love you!
 You know that Tom is a drug addict, right?

Adam Yeah, and you're a drunk.
 If you leave now, I promise I will never mention this to Eric.

Toby Adam –

Adam But only if you leave right now.

Toby But . . . but it's raining.

Adam grabs Toby's umbrella from Act One.

Adam Here. Take your shitty umbrella. I've been meaning to give it back to you anyway.

Toby Adam –

Adam Good night, Toby.

Young Man 1 Adam picked up his phone to call Eric.

Morgan But he stopped himself before he could dial.

Young Man 1 Why would he do that?

Morgan That night in Chicago, when he told Toby the story of what happened to him in Prague . . .

Young Man 1 He wanted to see how deeply he could draw Toby to him. He was surprised at how well it worked.

Morgan Perhaps it worked too well.

Young Man 1 Adam feared he might have been the unwitting author of Eric and Toby's breakup.

Morgan And *that* was the thought that caused him to put down his phone. Adam may have triumphed over Toby . . .

Young Man 1 But at what cost to Eric?

End of Scene One.

Autumn, 2016

Eric Autumn brought none of its usual joy to Eric Glass that year. He was forced to face the future alone.

Young Man 6 Toby had moved out a few days after their breakup.

Young Man 3 Walter was gone without a goodbye.

Young Man 4 Even Adam had vanished.

Young Man 5 And soon Eric's home would be gone, as well.

Young Man 7 Even his country was gone, having changed overnight like a sudden betrayal.

Eric Like Toby's betrayal.

Morgan Eric's plans for the future vanished overnight –

Eric – as if written in disappearing ink.

Young Man 8 Eric's first task was to find a new place to live.

Young Man 2 His next was to pack.

Eric He was daunted by both tasks.

Morgan And so it came as a great relief when Henry Wilcox knocked on Eric's door.

1. Eric's Apartment

Henry on Eric's doorstep, with a crystal wine decanter in his hands.

Henry Is this a bad time?

Eric No, not at all. In fact, you're aiding and abetting in some very important procrastination. I've been thinking about you, actually.

Henry You have?

Eric Yes, and wondering how you've been.

Henry I'm fine, thank you. This decanter belonged to Walter. It was his grandmother's, actually. Waterford. Manufactured in the mid-nineteenth century.

Eric It's beautiful.

Henry I want you to have it.

Eric Oh no, Henry, I couldn't.

Henry You can and you will. You were a good friend to him, especially at the end.

Eric I didn't know it was the end.

Henry Which is what made it all the more genuine. Please take it.

Eric Henry, it's way too expensive.

Henry It would mean a great deal to me if you accepted this as a gift from me in gratitude for your kindness.

Eric For you, then. And for Walter's memory.

Henry Thank you.

Eric Thank *you*.

Henry Are you moving?

Eric Yes, unfortunately. End of the year.

Henry Why 'unfortunately'?

Eric I lost the lease here.

Henry You've been renting this place?

Eric I love that you and Walter both thought I was secretly rich.

Henry I didn't think it was a secret.

Eric I'm terminally middle class.

Henry Where are you going?

Eric *That* is a very good question. I'm honestly feeling a little overwhelmed right now.

Henry Where's Toby in all of this?

Eric Burning in hell for all I care.

Henry Oh.

Eric Toby and I broke up.

Henry I'm sorry to hear that, Eric. You're going through some things right now, aren't you?

Eric Not like what you've been through.

Henry It doesn't have to be a competition.

Eric I thought to businessmen, everything was a competition.

Henry Not when it comes to suffering.

Eric Are you suffering, Henry?

Henry I really wish I hadn't used that word.

Eric Yes, but you have, so it's in play. Are you suffering?

Henry grows a sudden interest in the floor.

Henry He still gets mail. That's . . . well . . . anyway, I'm starting to realize just how much I depended on him.

Eric Funny. I'm starting to learn just how thoroughly undependable Toby was.

Henry I always liked the two of you together.

Eric Yeah, me too. But, you know, fuck him.
   Have you been lonely since Walter . . .?

Henry Work keeps me busy. And I have my sons.
   What's your plan, then? For the housing situation.

Eric The plan is to come up with a really good plan.

Henry Can you afford to buy?

Eric Maybe. If I look in the Bronx and it's 1977.

Henry All you have to do is fix your price, fix your
neighborhood and don't budge. I could put you in touch
with a broker, if you'd like.

Eric I would actually, thank you. I've had the wind taken
out of me. And then the election. I'm still reeling from
that, aren't you?

Henry Maybe not as much as you.

Eric It's actually a blessing that all of this is happening in
the fall.

Henry Why is that?

Eric There's just so much to do in the fall: new movies,
new plays, new books, dance, exhibitions. New York
Film Festival, City Ballet – the new Justin Peck piece is
coming up! – Restaurant Week, the BAM Next Wave
Festival alone, my God! New York is the perfect place
to waste your time and still maintain your dignity.

   Eric notices Henry smiling.

What?

Henry I'd forgotten how vivid you are.

Eric Me? No I'm not, I'm just – what do you do for fun?

Henry I work.

Eric And when that gets old . . .?

Henry It hasn't yet.

Eric Tell me one thing you do for fun.

Henry I read. History, mostly. Biographies, that sort of thing. Do you have plans tonight? I feel like having a nice dinner out. Do you want to come with me?

Eric Oh. I would love to.
   Oh shit, no! I have BAM tickets tonight.

Henry Ah. Another time, then.

Eric Yes. Actually, I have an extra ticket. What are your opinions on German expressionism?

Henry Oh. Well. I have no idea what that is but I'm pretty certain I hate it.

Eric How would you like to travel to Brooklyn with me tonight and broaden your horizons?

Henry Must they really stretch as far as Brooklyn?

Eric Boy, have you got a lot to learn, Henry Wilcox.

Henry And I suppose you think you're the person to teach me, Eric Glass.

Eric About certain things, yes.

Henry How long is this thing at BAM?

Eric Four hours.

Henry My God, that's obscene.

Eric But there's two intermissions.

Henry All in German?

Eric *Ja.*

Henry Fine, but I reserve the right to renegotiate at the first intermission.

2. *Various Locations*

Young Man 3 Thus the tyranny of the autumnal New York cultural scene continued to hold its sway over Eric Glass, infecting Henry Wilcox as well with its unrelenting demands.

Young Man 4 Henry's life was entrenched completely in commerce. Yet in the weeks that followed, Henry spent more time inside theatres, museums and concert halls than he had in decades.

Henry What the fuck are we watching here?

Eric This playwright is a genius.

Henry Says who?

Eric Well, he won the MacArthur award.

Henry Which means what, exactly?

Eric That he's a genius.

Henry But what makes him a genius?

Eric Beats me. I've never liked any of his plays.

Young Man 4 They frequented hot new restaurants in Bushwick that took no reservations and boasted of two-hour waits.

Young Man 3 Eric was appalled when Henry slipped the host a fifty-dollar bill. But his resistance faded when the action promptly landed them a table.

Henry Negotiation is like standing on opposing ends of a football field. Except, unlike in football, the goal of negotiation is to get the other guy to travel closer to your end of the field than you to his.

Eric You know that sports metaphors are completely lost on me, right?

Henry Decide what you want to hold on to but never let the other guy know what that is. Make him think everything is precious to you. That way he doesn't know what you're really willing to give up. Half of the things you ask for at the outset are there so you can make a show of letting go of them. And always be willing to walk away from the deal.

Morgan December arrived and Henry surprised both his sons by inviting Eric to join them for their annual visit to Peter Luger Steakhouse, the only reason Henry found a trip to Brooklyn was warranted.

3. Peter Luger Steakhouse

Eric, Henry, Charles and Paul at dinner.

Henry How is it you've lived in or around New York City all your life and you've never eaten here?

Eric It never occurred to me to travel outside of Manhattan for a steak. You can get a steak at any restaurant.

Paul } No, you cannot.
Charles } Not true at all.

Henry You can get grilled beef at any restaurant. But for a real steak, you have to come to Peter Luger's. What looks good to you?

Eric Everything. I can't decide.

Henry Let me order for the table, then. We'll start with the bacon. (It's not on the menu – you have to know to order it.) Four shrimp cocktails. Then we'll have two orders of the Porterhouse for two, medium rare. Also the prime rib, medium rare.

Charles, Paul *and* **Henry** Yes!

Paul Peter Luger Sauce, please.

Henry, Charles *and* **Paul** Yes!

Henry What else? Baked potatoes?

Charles, Paul *and* **Henry** Yes!

Charles And steak fries.

Henry, Paul *and* **Charles** Yes!

Paul And the German hash browns.

Henry, Charles *and* **Paul** Yes!

Henry And for dessert, a piece of cheesecake and the Holy Cow sundae.

Charles, Paul *and* **Henry** Yes!

Henry Do we feel that's enough?

Eric Maybe a vegetable?

Paul We're getting three.

Henry I think he means something green. Creamed spinach?

Eric Yes!

Henry That's how you order at Peter Luger's.

Young Man 5 It quickly became apparent to Charles and Paul that their father was engaged in a kind of fucking courtship with Eric.

Young Man 7 The brothers sat dumbfounded as Henry prompted Eric to prattle on about whatever fucking subjects he could devise.

Henry How's the apartment hunt coming along?

Eric Ugh, it's not. I just got outbid by a cash offer. Twenty per cent above asking. For a studio!

Henry This is why you need to have four or five other properties ready to make offers on next.

Eric I know, I know. I'm about to give up and start looking outside the city. Maybe you should just give me Walter's house.

Paul chokes on his drink.

Did I say something wrong?

Charles and Paul look at each other.

Don't tell me you sold it.

Paul ⎱ You can't have it.
Charles ⎰ It's rented.

Henry You don't want to live in the country, Eric. You're a city mouse through and through.

Eric I know. You're right. But it is tempting to think about leaving here. Well, if it ever becomes available, let me know. I'm at the point where I'm ready to throw in the towel and start raising alpacas.

Paul Alpacas?

Charles What the *fuck*?

Paul Yeah, *what* the fuck?

4. Elevator

Eric Thank you so much for dinner tonight, Henry. It was nice to . . . well, anyway, it was nice.

Henry It was my pleasure.

Eric Your sons think I'm a total weirdo.

Henry You *are* a total weirdo.

Eric I don't think they find it charming.

Henry I do.

Eric Do you ever worry about the future, Henry?

124

Henry No.

Eric How is that possible? Will you teach me?

Henry It's easy: just live through much worse and become a billionaire.

Eric Why didn't I think of that? It just feels as though the world is falling apart.

Henry The world has been falling apart since it began. That is what the world does: it falls, it's rebuilt. The same is true of people. You're stronger than you think.

The elevator dings.

Eric Do you want to come up to my place . . . for a bit?

Henry It's late. I should get to bed.

Eric Yeah. Yeah, okay. Well. Good night, Henry.

Henry Good night, Eric.

They shake hands. Henry exits.

Morgan Eric examined the decanter that Henry had brought him several weeks before.

Eric He thought about Walter and felt his loving embrace in that moment.

Morgan And in the next, longed for Henry's.

End of Scene Two.

SCENE THREE

Christmas Eve, 2016

Toby Toby rented a corner apartment on the 67th floor of a new construction in Hell's Kitchen. He bought clothes and furniture, he began working with a trainer –

Young Man 5 And started fucking his trainer.

Toby Toby was having the time of his life. Parties at the Public Hotel, dinners at the Polo Bar, threeways with Juilliard dancers.

Morgan But the emptiness he felt as a result of his breakup with Eric could not be easily pasted over by his libertine adventures.

Toby No, Toby was having fun.

Morgan But why was he having fun?

Toby Because he was young and handsome with a kick-ass fuck pad in the heart of New York City.

Morgan Because he is in pain.

Toby What the fuck is Toby in pain about?

Morgan Take your pick: the end of his relationship with Eric, Adam's rejection, the critical indifference to his work. There's a 'why' behind every action. And very likely a 'why' behind every 'why'.

Toby It was Toby and Eric's tradition to attend the matinee of *The Nutcracker* every Christmas Eve with Eric's friends.

Morgan But Toby was disinvited this year.

Toby Fine, then. It's a stupid ballet anyway. Toby thought of calling Adam.

Morgan But Adam was in Brazil with the director Tom Durrell.

Toby Fine, then. Toby called Tristan.

Tristan As if, bitch.

Toby Toby called the Jasons.

Jason 2 Oh my God, Toby!

Jason 1 Have you seen the new sonograms?

Jason 1 *and* **Jason 2** The baby's getting so big.

Toby Toby hung up on the Jasons.

Morgan Who then does Toby turn to?

Toby No one. Toby treats himself to a meal at Eleven Madison Park.

Young Man 4 Thanks for the tip. Merry Christmas!

Toby He goes home and . . . he goes home and opens an expensive bottle of wine.

Morgan And then what?

Toby He drinks it.

Morgan And then what?

Toby It tastes good.

Morgan And then what?
  Then he feels an overwhelming spasm of loneliness that, on this night, the wine could not alleviate.

Toby No.

Morgan And that is how he found himself online, seeking out less complicated companionship.

Toby Is Toby about to get laid? Because I'm totally down with that.

Morgan Toby was stopped short by the profile.
  Was it him?

Toby Who?

Morgan But no, it couldn't be.

Toby Who are you talking about?

Morgan But that face. It was the same face, give or take.

Toby Whose face?

Morgan Toby knew he had to have this boy, if only for one night. If only to pretend. Toby texted the number on the ad and, two hours later . . . Leo appeared at his door.

1. Toby's Apartment

Young Man 1 becomes Leo.

Toby Hi.

Leo Hey.

Toby Thanks for coming on such short notice.

Leo Yeah.

Toby Can I get you a drink?

Leo I'm good.

He goes to the window, staring out.

Toby Great view, huh? You can see the whole city.

Leo Cool.

Toby reaches for Leo. Leo pulls away.

Toby Sorry, I – I've never done this before.

Leo With a guy?

Toby Oh God no. That ship has sailed. It's just my first time, you know . . .

Morgan Paying for it.

Toby So how does this work, exactly?

Leo You tell me what you want, I'll tell you if I do it.

Toby I wanna fuck you.

Leo Okay.

Toby How / much?

Leo looks around the apartment then decides –

Leo Two hundred.

Toby Okay.

Leo You have condoms?

Toby Oh. Um –

Leo I brought some.

Toby I'm neg for what it's worth.

Leo Me too but I don't fuck raw.

Toby Right. I wasn't trying to not use them. I was just saying that you have nothing to fear from me. How old are you?

Leo Old enough.

He starts undressing. He then realizes Toby isn't.

Are you okay?

Toby Yeah. It's just that you're really beautiful, you know that? Can I kiss you?

Leo That's more intimate than I like.

Toby I'm about to fuck you.

Leo I know.

Toby But kissing is too intimate?

Leo Yes.

Toby I'll pay an extra hundred if you let me kiss you.

A beat.

Leo Okay.

Toby approaches Leo, takes a moment, then kisses him. Leo quickly pulls away. It's a two-dollar kiss at best. Leo continues undressing.

Toby What's your name?

Leo Leo.

Toby Can I call you 'Adam'?

Leo Why?

Toby You just look like an 'Adam' to me.

Leo Sure, whatever.

Toby Will you . . . will you tell me you love me?

Leo What?

Toby I'll pay you another hundred.
Please.

Leo looks at Morgan for help.

Morgan Tell him.

Leo I love you.

Toby Say, 'I love you, Toby.'

Leo I love you, Toby.

Toby Say it again. Make me believe it.

Leo I love you, Toby.

Toby I love you, Adam. Again.

Leo I love you, Toby.

A beat, then:

Toby Let's go to bed.

Lights shift then rise on Toby's bed. Toby is asleep. Leo sits up, staring out Toby's massive windows.

Morgan Our society does not concern itself with the very poor. We pretend we do because we know that we should. But to most, even the best intentioned, the poor are invisible, and only to be considered by the statistician or the poet. This story so far deals with the middle class, give or take, and even with those who feel obliged to pretend that they are upper class. The boy Leo was neither. He was born, he was raised, and he lived in poverty. It was not the romantic poverty of fiction, but rather the poverty of fact. Leo was not yet at the abyss, but he could see it, and at times people he knew had dropped into it and counted no more.

Leo sat in Toby's bed, looking at the skyline that – what?

Leo Shimmered?

Morgan Yes. That shimmered before him. He had never been this high up in the city before. He couldn't help being . . . what?

Leo Dazzled by the view.

Morgan Leo knew he should dress and go home, that the trip would be a long one at this hour.

Leo He'd forgotten to ask for cash upfront.

Morgan Rookie mistake, not to be repeated.

Leo Leo would have to wake him to get his money. And that got scary sometimes, even with the nice ones. The need to ask made him feel . . . well, like a whore.

Morgan But sitting in this warm, comfortable bed, looking out at the city, relaxed and even sleepy after his unexpected orgasm –

Leo Leo took a breath and pretended for one, two, three seconds that he belonged here, in this apartment, in this man's bed.

Morgan The city was hypnotic from way up here, safely above the chaos.

Leo From this great height, in this warm bed, for just this moment, Leo was safe.

Morgan For once, he could stare at the tiger –

Leo – and not fear its teeth.

Toby stirs awake.

Toby Did I fall asleep?

Leo Just for a minute.

Toby What are you doing?

Leo Getting dressed.

Toby What's the rush?

Leo It's late.

Toby Come here for a second.

Leo I should go.

Toby Stay.

Leo It's late.

Toby So stay.

Leo I can't. Really. So . . .

Toby Yeah?

Morgan His money.

Toby Oh! Right, sorry. What's the damage?

Leo Four hundred.

Toby What?!

Morgan With the extras.

Toby Oh. Right.

He takes a wad of cash, hands it over.

Leo Thank you.

Toby Thank *you*.

He notices a small book in Leo's pocket, snatches it.

Toby What book are you reading? (*Reading the cover.*) *The Open Road.*

Leo Please give it back.

Toby What's it about?

Leo It's just a bunch of old poems about nature and shit.

Toby Read one to me.

Leo No.

Toby Oh go on. Read me one of your favorites. Please?
I'll pay you a hundred dollars to read me a poem right now.

Leo opens the book, looks for his favorite and reads:

Leo 'With lifted / feet –'

Toby Wait, what's the poem called?

Leo Oh. Um . . .
Going Downhill on a Bicycle.
'With lifted feet hands still I am poised, and down the hill dart with heedful mind the air goes by in a wind –'
This is stupid, I can't do this.

Morgan helps Leo understand the verse.

Morgan
With lifted feet, hands still,
I am poised, and down the hill
Dart, with heedful mind;
The air goes by in a wind.

133

Leo
    Swifter and yet more swift,
    Till the heart, with a mighty lift,
    Makes the lungs laugh, the throat cry . . .
    'O bird, see: see, bird: I fly!

    'Is this, is this your joy,
    O bird, then I, though a boy,
    For a golden moment share
    Your feathery life in air.'

Morgan Well done.

Toby Thank you.

    Toby hands over a hundred-dollar bill.

Leo You're funny.

Toby Why do you say that?

Leo You act like we're friends.

Toby I make friends easily.

Leo I don't.

Toby So go.

Leo Yeah, okay.

Toby That wasn't me kicking you out.

Leo I was leaving anyway.

Toby I just want to make you feel comfortable here.

Leo You have.

Toby Can I see you again?

Leo Call me whenever you wanna fuck.

Toby Right. Yeah. Here . . . my card.

    He pulls out a card, hands it to Leo.

Leo You have cards?

Toby Classy, no?

Morgan 'Toby Darling, Child of Privilege.'

Toby Keep it. In case you ever need me.

Leo Why would I need you?

Toby I don't know. Just in case you do.

Leo slides the card into his book, heads to the door.

You sure you don't want to stay over?

A moment, then Leo comes back into the room, approaches Toby and gives him a hundred-dollar kiss.

Leo Merry Christmas.

Leo exits.

Morgan It was without question the most unexpected Christmas Eve of Toby's life.

Young Man 1 But what Toby did not know – what he could not have known – was that he would only live to see one more.

Silence, then:

Toby I'm sorry, what?

Young Man 1 Toby would only live to see one more Christmas.

Morgan Are you certain?

Young Man 1 Yes.

Toby What the fuck are you talking about?

Morgan That's an awfully big decision to make, with still so much of the story left to tell.

Young Man 1 It's the reason we're telling it.

Morgan Are you absolutely certain?

Young Man 1 Yes.

Young Man 4 But why?

Young Man 8 How does it happen?

Young Man 2 I don't know how I feel about this.

Young Man 6 Maybe we should wait before deciding on this.

Morgan You may want to change your mind as the story progresses.

Young Man 1 You don't know how desperately I wish I could.

Toby Don't I get any say in this?

Young Man 1 Two days after Christmas, Henry attempted to solve Eric's housing dilemma.

Toby But wait . . .

End of Scene Three.

SCENE FOUR

December 2016

1. An Empty Apartment

Eric Oh wow!

Henry You like it?

Eric I love it!

Henry And it comes with a key.

Eric Well, I should hope so.

Henry No, numbskull. A key to the park.

Eric Gramercy Park?

Henry The one and only.

Eric I can't afford to buy this.

Henry The thing is that it's not for sale, it's just to rent. But you can afford it if you want it.

Eric How is that possible?

Henry Because I own it. What's the rent on your place right now?

Eric Five hundred and seventy-five dollars.

Henry Jesus, you've been getting away with murder. I'll charge you a thousand.

Eric Henry, are you sure?

Henry Only if you commit to buying something next year.

Eric Deal! Thank you! My very own apartment off of Gramercy Park. I feel like a Henry James character.

Henry I do have one other idea to run past you.

Eric You're just full of great ideas today, aren't you?

Henry I'm going to be leaving for Paris just after the New Year.

Eric Oh. How long will you be gone?

Henry Possibly through the spring.

Eric Oh. I see. I'm . . . I'm actually sad to hear that.

Henry Yes, well . . . I was wondering . . . before we settle on this apartment . . .

Eric Yes?

Henry Why don't you come with me?

Eric To Paris?

Henry For the winter.

Eric Oh. Well . . . I have my work.

Henry I wasn't sure how much time you could afford to take off.

Eric I mean, I have vacation time, but not four months' worth.

Henry No. No, of course not.

Eric And besides, with the Inauguration coming up, I'm going to be really busy. We're running campaigns against the cabinet appointments, mobilizing protests –

Henry The thing is . . . these past few weeks, I've . . . I've grown very . . . I've gotten used to having you around and I don't see why that can't continue while I'm away.

Eric Jasper would kill me if I took time off right now.

Jasper Damned right I would.

Henry Jasper's world will spin without you, Eric. Mine perhaps will not. I'm going to miss you. And I don't want to. So why should I?

2. *Eric and Jasper*

Jasper What do you mean, 'leave of absence'?

Eric I haven't taken a vacation in over a year.

Jasper And you're not getting one for a very long time. Vacations are canceled until at least the '18 midterms, don't you understand that?

Eric I have given you so much over the years. I'm asking you for two weeks for myself.

Jasper This isn't about me, Eric. It's about our country.

Eric My taking just a little time off is not going to make any difference. The world will spin without me.

Young Man 8 The next day, movers came to take Eric's things to his new place off Gramercy Park. What didn't fit went into storage.

Young Man 1 All that was left were Toby's possessions, which Eric had carefully boxed up, berating himself for doing Toby's work for him.

Morgan And so, on New Year's Eve, the former partners met for their final goodbye.

3. Eric and Toby's Apartment

Toby sorts through a stack of books. Other moving boxes surround him.

Toby Why didn't I get a Kindle? Shoulda got a Kindle. Of course, you can't take Kindles into the bathtub. But then again, you can't take *Infinite Jest* into the bathtub, either.

Eric You've never read *Infinite Jest*.

Toby Neither have you.

Eric Yes, but I don't tell people that I have.

Toby That was once at a party and I was talking to Zadie Smith. She made me nervous. I lie when I'm nervous.

Eric You drink when you're nervous. You lie when you drink.

Toby Are you intentionally trying to pick a fight?

Eric Yes. You also left behind a box of your parents' things.

Toby looks at the box, then ignores it, diving back into his books.

Eric Toby, I have plans I have to get to.

Toby You hate New Year's Eve. Where are you going?

Eric Henry invited me over.

Toby Henry? Why would anyone want to spend New Year's Eve with Henry Wilcox?

Eric I like Henry.

Toby What is there to like?

Eric I found enough in you to keep me occupied for seven years.

Toby cautiously circles the box of his parents' things, not daring to go near it.

I need you to know how sad this makes me.

Toby We were going to have to move out eventually.

Eric Not the apartment, Toby. Us. What happened to us?

Toby We just . . . we grew apart.

Eric But Toby, you haven't grown.

Toby Okay, you know what? Keep the books, I don't need them. Well this was a real nice clambake. See ya around.

Eric Aren't you going to take your parents' things?

Toby Toss 'em, I don't want them.

Eric I don't think you mean that.

Toby Trust me, I do. They did fuck-all for me while they were alive. I'm supposed to schlep their shit around for the rest of my life? Fuck 'em. I don't need what's in that box.

Eric You are setting the stage for one miserable life, Toby.

Toby Oh, fuck you, Eric. At least I'm living my life. You'd have died of old age in this apartment if they hadn't taken it from you, eaten by your cats. Your whole life has been one safe move after another. So I don't want to hear from you / that I –

Eric Henry asked me to go to Paris with him.

Toby He did not.
Did he?

Eric *Pourquoi pas?*

Toby You're not seriously thinking of going, are you?

Eric Why shouldn't I go to Paris if I can?

Toby Are you fucking Henry?

Eric Are you fucking Adam?

Toby You bet your ass I am. It is the best sex of my life. You've never heard sounds like the kind that kid makes when I fuck him.

Eric Mazel tov, Toby. I'm so happy for you both. Maybe his parents can adopt you, too.

Toby Fuck you, Eric.

He turns to leave.

Eric Wait – please.
I love you, Toby. And the fact that you don't seem to understand how badly I'm hurting right now hurts me even more. Did you ever love me?

Toby I mean, obviously.

Eric seems to have an epiphany.

What?

Eric No one ever taught you what that means, did they?

Toby What the fuck are you talking about?

Eric Take these things your parents left behind.

Toby No thanks.

Morgan Toby stopped at the door and looked back at the apartment that had been his home for the past seven years.

Young Man 2 The only real home he'd known since childhood.

Young Man 4 The home in which he wrote his novel *Loved Boy*.

Young Man 5 The home in which he and Eric had been engaged.

Young Man 6 Toby looked at the apartment, longing for a connection with the past –

Young Man 7 – wanting to tell Eric how much he meant to him.

Young Man 8 And so in that moment, Toby said –

Toby See you around, then.

Morgan No, Toby apologized. Toby asked Eric to take him back.

Toby No, he shut the door on the past and he went out and lived his life.

Young Man 1 If only Toby had decided to stay in that moment. He could have changed the fate that awaited him sooner than he could possibly imagine.

Toby All right, fuck the both of you with your fucking dire warnings and prognostications. In fact, fuck all of you. Toby says goodbye, Toby leaves his boxes, and Toby goes to a killer party that none of you could get invited to. That's what Toby does.

Morgan Why didn't Toby take his parents' things?

Toby Because he doesn't want them.

Morgan What is in there that scares Toby so much?

Toby I don't care!

Morgan You've heard the fate that awaits you. If there was any hope of changing it, why wouldn't you take it?

Toby Because I don't believe that is my fate. I'm not telling that story and I'm not looking in those fucking boxes.

Morgan If we are to learn what we mean to each other, we must first examine what we mean to *ourselves*. And we must be fearless and honest in that attempt –

Toby Yeah, I'm gonna call bullshit on that. Why should we listen to you lecture us about fearlessness and honesty when you were never honest about yourself in your lifetime?

The Lads jeer at him.

Young Man 3 } Way out of line!
Young Man 5 } That is so unfair!

Toby Why is it unfair? He never once told the world who he was.

Young Man 1 We are telling this story today because the world knows who Morgan was.

Toby No, he left it for the world to discover after he died. But while he was alive, he was anything but fearless and honest. (*To Morgan.*) Isn't that right, Morgan? The great E. M. Forster, beloved by all the world. And secretly the gayest daisy in the field. (*To the Lads.*) E. M. Forster, whose two most famous words were 'only connect', could not do so himself. He didn't have sex until he was thirty-eight. He lived with his mother until she died. He locked himself in the closet all his life. (*To

143

Morgan.) You never told the truth about yourself so why the fuck should we listen to you now?

Morgan Because you now have the chance to be honest, which is something I was never given.

Toby You had countless opportunities to be honest. You lived until 1970. You watched the moon landing, for God's sake. You were alive during Stonewall. The world changed because people were brave. You weren't.

Young Man 1 Morgan wrote *Maurice* in 1912. That wasn't brave?

Toby No! Because he hid it from the world for fifty-six years. (*To Morgan.*) Just imagine what would have happened if you had published a gay novel in your lifetime! You might have toppled mountains. You might have even saved lives. But you didn't do that. (*To the Lads.*) Morgan had his chance to be honest and he fucking squandered it. He left others to do the heavy lifting and then he slipped it in at the end. (*To Morgan.*) And because of that, you're fucking irrelevant. You're just books on a shelf gathering dust. You're a Merchant Ivory film.

Young Man 3 I like Merchant Ivory films.

Morgan I'm trying to save you.

Toby *I don't need you to save me!!* I don't need anything from you. You have nothing to teach us because you can't possibly understand what it's like to live in freedom, to demand choices for yourself. Toby doesn't have to do anything he doesn't want to. He doesn't have to listen to you, he doesn't have to look in any boxes. Toby's gonna fuck who he wants and live how he likes because that is his right as a gay man in the world you did *nothing* to help build.

He exits.

Young Man 1 Morgan.

Silence.

Morgan The thing is, Lads: he isn't wrong.

The Lads protest.

He didn't say it as kindly as he could have. But he said it nonetheless: there's nothing I can teach you that you don't already know. You understand your story better than I could ever hope to. I think it would be best for me to leave you.

The Lads protest.

Young Man 4 Morgan, no. You are essential to our story.

Morgan No, lads. *You* are essential to your story. I like to believe I was helpful to you as you started it. But I cannot help you finish it. It isn't my right to. The past must be faced. It must be learned from. But it cannot be revised. I had my time. Now it is yours.

The Lads protest.

Young Man 1 There's still so much you haven't told us. There's still so much we don't know.

Morgan You have everything you need. Trust in that. Trust in yourselves.

Oh, my lads, how I do love you. You have allowed me to see . . . what I could not live. What a gift! I think your lives are beautiful. And I know at what cost they have come. Tell your story bravely. It is a story worth telling. Take care of yourselves. Take care of each other. (*Re: Toby.*) Take care of him most especially.

I am certain we shall find each other again, by and by.

Morgan exits.
  A long, uncertain silence.
  Eventually, we find ourselves back where we started: with the Young Men gathered together and

Young Man 1 on the periphery of the group. Then, finally:

Young Man 1 He has a story to tell.

Young Man 8 It is banging around inside him, aching to come out.

Young Man 3 But how does he continue?

Young Man 4 He opens his favorite novel –

Young Man 5 – hoping to find inspiration –

Young Man 6 – hoping to find guidance from its author.

Young Man 2 But they are just words on a page –

Young Man 7 – written down a hundred years ago.

Young Man 9 And their author now refuses his summons.

Young Man 1 He must tell his story himself.

Young Man 1 sets down his copy of Howards End.

Young Man 1 Paris . . . in the wintertime . . . is . . . what?

Young Man 3 Cold.

Young Man 2 Grey?

Young Man 1 No. What else?

Young Man 4 Paris in the wintertime is . . .

Young Man 6 Paris in the wintertime is . . .

Young Man 8 Quiet.

Young Man 7 Simple?

Young Man 1 Not quite it.

Young Man 5 Paris in the wintertime is . . .

Young Man 1 Paris in the wintertime is . . . underrated.

Eric Paris in the wintertime is *vastly* underrated. Songs will never be written extolling its virtues. But Eric Glass found it enchanting.

Young Man 1 He visited Henry every weekend that winter.

Young Man 7 He skipped the Women's March.

Young Man 8 He missed the protests against the travel ban.

Young Man 4 But he did read Proust in the Tuileries –

Young Man 3 – and Hemingway in Café Charlot.

Young Man 1 Eric and Henry grew closer, fonder.

Young Man 6 They traveled to St-Tropez together when the weather warmed.

Eric America seethed and boiled but Eric's heart slowly healed.

Young Man 3 Henry Wilcox returned to New York in May, where his new West Village townhouse was finally ready to move into. Eric spent many evenings there.

End of Scene Four.

SCENE FIVE

Spring 2017

1. Henry's Townhouse

Young Man 5 One night in late May, Henry invited his sons over for dinner.

Young Man 7 They were chagrined when they arrived to discover that Eric was in the kitchen preparing the meal.

Young Man 3 But their resistance faded once they tasted his cooking.

Paul Not bad.

Charles Not bad.

Young Man 3 Deep into the meal's third bottle of wine, Paul unadvisedly opened his mouth.

Paul And on top of all the other bullshit I have to deal with, I've got this fucking tenant at Walter's house busting my balls about when he can get his deposit back.

Charles Paul, maybe tonight's not the –

Paul I'm like: I've got a three-hundred-million-dollar condo in Queens in the middle of construction – I don't have time to deal with this penny ante bullshit.

Charles Paul.

Paul I don't know why you hang on to that house, Pop. You should just do us all a favor and sell the fucking thing.

Eric What's happening at Walter's house?

Paul Nothing for you to be concerned with. (*To Henry.*) They scorched the ceiling in the kitchen with a grease fire. They let their dog piss and shit all over the place. They almost killed the cherry tree by hitting it with a pickup truck.

Eric They damaged the cherry tree?

Paul This isn't your concern.

Eric Walter loved that tree. Has anyone gone up to look at it?

Paul It's a fucking tree.

Eric No, but to Walter that tree was . . . Henry, why don't you and I go? I'd love to see the house.

Charles Pop's very busy.

Paul Pop doesn't have time / to go up –

Henry Why do you want to see the house?

Eric Walter told me so much about it, I'd love to finally see it. And I do miss Walter.

After a moment:

Henry I understand.

Young Man 1 As you drive out of the city on certain roads, a miraculous thing happens. At a certain point where the Bronx meets Westchester, the city suddenly stops –

Eric – like a switch has been flipped –

Young Man 1 – and the country begins.

Young Man 4 The closer they got to the house, the less inclined Henry was toward conversation.

Young Man 3 Eric watched him tense with every mile, Henry's fingers tightly gripping the wheel.

Young Man 4 They drove up the last few miles in silence, eventually turning onto a state road, then a county road and then a meandering country lane. Eric's chest heaved with eager anticipation.

Young Man 3 It was late May and the trees were already lush with leaves, the countryside was young and fresh and expectant. Finally, when Eric felt he could stand the wait no longer, Henry slowed the car.

2. Walter's House

Eric Are we here?

Henry The property is just through those trees.

Eric Aren't we pulling in?

Henry The keys are at the caretaker's. It's just up the road.

Eric Henry, stop the car! I want to get out.

Henry Why?

Eric I want to explore.
  Is that okay?

Henry It'll just be half an hour.

Eric But I'm here now.

A moment, then Henry smiles.

Henry Go on. I won't be long.

*Eric stands alone for a moment. He breathes the air.
The sound of birdsong can be faintly heard. It grows
and increases its presence over time. Then the sound of
a breeze rustling through the leaves of countless trees.*
*And then, ever so slowly, the house begins to
appear, like a great ship emerging through the mist,
silently imposing its mystical presence upon us.
Eventually it fills the stage, dwarfing Eric, clearly and
insistently revealing itself to us. The house as Walter
described it, as it has haunted Eric's imagination. We
also see the grounds surrounding it. The cherry tree in
front and the rolling meadow beyond. The color green
is omnipresent: in the grass, in the trees, in the brilliant
morning sunlight diffusing itself through all the many
leaves. It is a wondrous sight.*
As this is happening:

Eric The car turned away, and Eric stood by the hedgerow
that protected the property from the road and he stepped
for the first time onto the grounds. It was as if a curtain
had risen. It was exactly as Walter had described. The
meadow rolling down to the grove of trees. The air, filled
with breezes and birdsong. The cherry tree with the pig's

teeth stuck into the trunk, its branches covering the porch with shade. The pink blossoms from earlier in the spring still dancing around in the grass. He was struck by the fertility of the soil; he had seldom been in a garden where the flowers looked so healthy. Even the weeds were intensely green. Why had the tenants fled from all this beauty? For Eric had already decided that this place was beautiful. And then, there before him was the house itself, standing as it had for centuries. It wasn't at all what he expected. In fact, he was momentarily disappointed. To anyone else, it was simply a house. But Eric knew it was Walter's house. And because of that, it found it beautiful. Eric thought of Walter, and the story of his friend Peter who came here to die, of all the young men who came here to find peace in their final days. He thought of all the men who died in those years and what they might have become, what the world would look like today had they been allowed to end their story on their own terms. Eric wondered what his life would be like if he had not been robbed of a generation of mentors, of poets, of friends, and perhaps even lovers. Eric breathed and filled his lungs with the past. It stretched before him now, limitless – the past and the present, mingling together inside this house, inside him.

Young Man 1 Eric approached the house.

Young Man 3 He laid his hand upon the door.

Young Man 6 It opened.

Young Man 2 The house was not locked up after all.

Young Man 4 Eric walked inside.

A Man enters.

Man Walter, is that you?

Eric No, I . . .

Man I'm sorry. I thought you were Walter for a moment. You have his way of walking around the house.

Eric I'm Eric.

Man Eric Glass?

Eric Yes, that's right. How did you –

Suddenly, the various rooms of the house start to fill with young men. The house is filled with ghosts.

Man It's so nice to finally meet you. We've heard so much about you.

Eric Me? Who are you?

Man I'm Peter.

Eric Peter?

Man Peter West. I'm a friend of Walter's. Welcome home, Eric.

End of Part One.

Part Two

Prologue

Eric The house . . .
  The house was . . .

Young Man 6 The house was . . .

Young Man 5 The house was definitely . . .

Young Man 1 The house was built in 1790. It was as old as the nation. Henry Wilcox was its sixth owner.

Young Man 3 It was built by a veteran of the Revolutionary War –

Young Man 4 – a farmer, who once briefly served in the New York State Legislature.

Young Man 2 It later belonged to an abolitionist family in the mid-nineteenth century –

Young Man 5 – and was briefly used as a safe house for escaped slaves along the Underground Railroad.

Young Man 6 The family's oldest son was killed at Antietam –

Young Man 8 – and their youngest a year later at Gettysburg.

Young Man 7 Franklin Roosevelt once attended a party here while campaigning for governor.

Young Man 2 The family who owned it at that time later lost a son in Bastogne –

Young Man 4 – but his two brothers survived the war.

Young Man 1 Henry Wilcox bought the house in 1987 from the youngest of those brothers –

Young Man 4 And in the fall of 1988, Henry's partner Walter brought their friend Peter West to die in the house.

Young Man 6 Across two centuries, countless wars –

Young Man 8 – booms and busts –

Young Man 2 – births, funerals –

Young Man 3 – weddings, christenings.

Young Man 4 Peter's death was the very first inside its walls.

Young Man 5 It would not be the last.

Young Man 7 In the intervening years, countless more men followed in Peter's footsteps.

Eric How could this house not be haunted?

Young Man 1 Eric stood in the front hallway, reeling from what he had just seen –

Young Man 5 – what he had just experienced.

Eric What he had just imagined?

Young Man 2 Was it possible?

Young Man 7 Had he seen them?

Young Man 8 Felt their presence?

Young Man 3 Eric had built this place up so much in his mind –

Eric Could it all just be his imagination?

Young Man 1 Then, before Eric had time to answer that question, Henry appeared in the doorway.

Act One

Spring 2017–Summer 2017

SCENE ONE

1. Walter's House

Henry You got in.

Eric The door was unlocked.

Henry That figures. Is it what you thought it would be?

Eric I don't know anymore.

Henry It's not all that much to speak of, as far as houses go. More an accumulation of problems at this point. The stairs need to be rebuilt. The furnace replaced. Probably a new roof soon enough.

Eric Do you look for flaws in people the way you do in houses?

Henry Houses hide their flaws much better than people.

Eric Do I have flaws, Henry?

Henry Oh boy, do you ever.

Eric What are my flaws?

Henry You want me to tell you your flaws?

Eric I could tell you yours, if you'd like.

Henry No, I wouldn't.
  You can't take a compliment.

Eric I don't think that's true.

Henry You undervalue yourself.

Eric Isn't that the same thing?

Henry It's the reason for the thing.

Eric Is that all?

Henry You're overly romantic, you're wildly impractical, you're stubborn as hell.

Eric That last one is rich coming from you.

Henry And, worst of all, you refuse to believe that you're beautiful.
    Listen, Eric . . . I know how hard these last few months have been for you.

Eric You have no idea how much you've helped me.

Henry I think, in fact, I do. Because you've helped me just as much. And I've been thinking: what role can we play in each other's lives going forward?

Eric You've been thinking that?

Henry I think about you more than you know.
    And . . . I wondered . . . if you would want to marry me.

Young Man 8 Twist!

Henry My God, I've rendered Eric Glass speechless.

Eric You want to marry . . . me?

Henry Yes.

Eric But . . . why?

Henry You make me smile. Contrary to what most people think, I do like to smile.

Eric I think you have a very nice smile.

Henry I'm glad you think so because you've been the author of all my recent smiles.
    I want you in my life, Eric.

Eric I *am* in your life.

Henry I want you fully in it. I can provide you with the freedom to find meaning in your life. To become the man you're meant to be. All I ask is that you share your spirit with me.

Gentle, rolling thunder in the distance.

Eric Can I think about it?

If Henry's disappointed, he covers it up.

Henry Of course.

Eric It's just that it's a big decision and you caught me by surprise.

Henry You don't have to explain yourself, Eric. Take all the time you need.

More thunder.

We should probably head back.

Eric But we just got here.

Henry I saw what I needed to see. That tenant is definitely not getting his deposit back.

Eric I was hoping we could spend the day here. Walter told me so much but it feels –

Henry I'd like to beat the storm.

Eric Okay, Henry. We can go.

Eric exits. Henry stands there, a moment, looking at the house. Then:
   Young Man 3 becomes Young Henry and Young Man 4 becomes Young Walter.

Young Henry I can't see the house.

Young Walter Almost there!

Young Henry I think we're lost.

Young Walter No, it's –
Yes! Here – just beyond these trees.
Oh wow! This isn't at all what I expected.

Young Henry It's smaller than I thought it would be.

Young Walter Yeah, but just look at it! It's perfect. Look at that cherry tree – isn't it beautiful? And wow – that meadow! Come on! Let's go explore the property.

Young Henry We should probably wait here.

Young Walter I'll be right back.

Young Henry Don't go too far.
Walter!

Henry Walter.

Young Walter runs off. Henry and Young Henry are alone.

Young Henry It *is* beautiful, isn't it?

Young Walter comes running back on, carrying a bundle of wildflowers in his hands.

Young Walter Look at these flowers. And there's an old barn. We could turn it into a dining pavilion.
This is it, Henry. This is our house. I can feel it. Don't you feel it, too?

Young Henry does not – or cannot – answer.

Is this what you want, Henry?

Young Henry I want to live.

Young Walter We can do that here. Look –

Young Walter shows Young Henry his bouquet. Young Henry sneezes.

You'll get used to it.

Henry sneezes.

Eric Henry!

Henry Coming, Eric.

Young Man 1 And so Henry Wilcox locked the door to Walter's house and walked away from it, determined he would never see it again.

End of Scene One.

SCENE TWO

Spring 2017

Young Man 6 Eric decided to introduce Henry to his friends.

Young Man 8 He planned one of his famous Sunday brunches in Henry's sumptuous new West Village townhouse –

Young Man 6 – privately fretting that Henry might not do well under the glare of their careful inspection.

Young Man 7 And so when Jasper asked if he could bring his new boyfriend –

Tucker Tucker!

Young Man 7 – Eric happily agreed.

Young Man 2 They arrived an hour late.

1. Henry's Townhouse

Eric, Henry, Tristan, Jasper, Jason 1, Jason 2 and Tucker.

Jasper Tucker's an artist. We met at Coachella. He makes the most incredible . . . Tell them what you call it.

Tucker Faux-art.

Tristan What is 'faux-art'?

Jason 2 Like out of Vietnamese noodles?

Tucker False art.

Tristan Meaning what?

Tucker Meaning that it isn't real.

Eric Like an illusion?

Tucker You could say that.

Jason 2 Like David Copperfield?

Jasper It's real in the sense you can see it, touch it.

Tristan Are we talking sculpture? Paintings?

Tucker Paintings.

Eric (*attempting to understand*) False paintings.

Tucker Yes.

Tristan But what makes them false?

Jasper Ah! Here's the genius part. Tell them.

Tucker You can tell them. They're your friends.

Jasper Yes, but it's your art. You should tell them.

Tucker I want to hear you describe it. It turns me on.

Jasper and Tucker start to make out.

Tristan Oh for fuck's sake, just tell us!

Jasper It's false because he doesn't mean it.

A beat, then:

Eric What do you mean, 'He doesn't mean it'?

Jasper They're false.

Tristan You've lost me.

Jasper Okay, here: take a look at Tucker's Instagram.

Tucker hands the Jasons his phone.

Jason 1 But these are beautiful.

Jason 2 Wow, look at that one.

Tristan That's incredible.

Eric Henry.

Henry Let's have a look.

They hand the phone to Henry.

Henry You painted this?

Tucker Which one are you looking at?

Henry This landscape.

Tucker Yeah, I did that last week.

Henry And this portrait . . . ?

Tucker My grandmother.

Henry You're a Rembrandt, kid. The shading, the depth of color.

They get to one that's . . .

Eric Whoa!

Henry Is that you, Jasper?

Tristan Jasper?

Jason 2 There's a portrait of Jasper?

Eric Not a portrait.

Henry A nude.

Tristan What?

Jason 1 You're kidding.

Jason 2 Let me see.

They all gather around Henry.

Jason 1 That's . . .

Jason 2 Oh my.

Tristan Jasper, your dick is not that big.

Eric Who's your gallerist?

Jasper Tucker doesn't sell them.

Henry So what does he do with them?

Tucker I burn them.

Jason 1	You're kidding.
Tristan	Stop.
Eric	You burn these?
Jason 2	Why?

Eric But they're beautiful.

Tucker Beautiful but meaningless.

Eric Now wait . . . You cannot tell me there is no meaning in this portrait of your grandmother. Her eyes are so soulful, her face so kind. How is that untrue?

Tucker Because my grandmother's a fucking cunt, dude.

Jasper False art!

Tristan So all of your paintings are . . .

Tucker The world as you would like me to show it to you.

Tristan I *knew* Jasper's dick was not that big.

Henry Why not just paint what is true?

Tucker Because no one wants the truth anymore.

Eric People are desperate for the truth.

Tucker People want the illusion of truth. They want a story that validates their beliefs: about themselves, their nation, the world.

Henry 'When the legend becomes fact, print the legend.'

Eric *Man Who Shot Liberty Valance!*

Henry Gold star!
   Why do you take a picture before you destroy the painting? And more to the point: why do you then post it on social media?

Tucker To show the world / what is false and –

Henry Nah, I'm not buying it. I think you want the credit for having made it without taking responsibility for what it means. That portrait of your grandmother may not be 'true' but it certainly is beautiful and / in painting it –

Tucker That's not who / she is, though.

Henry Let me finish, Tucker. And in painting it, you've taken something that is ugly to you and you've made it beautiful. If that doesn't demonstrate the genuine power of art, I don't know what does. I don't think you mistrust beauty, Tucker. I think you mistrust the truth. I think you mistrust yourself.

Tucker Hot!

Eric The conversation continued as Eric went to the kitchen to make coffee. He listened as Henry engaged his friends about their lives, their work, their passions. In that moment, Eric glimpsed the future that was opening to him. But as he returned with the cookies –

Jason 1 Wait, wait, wait! You're a Republican?

Jasper Eric, did you know about this?

Eric Well, I mean . . . I knew that Henry was relatively conservative, / but –

Jasper And that he gave money to the party last year, including to the nominee?

Eric You donated to his campaign?

Henry I did.

Eric Why?

Henry He asked.

Tristan You know him?

Henry Yeah, of course I do.

Eric And you gave him money?

Henry I'm a Republican. This can't be such a surprise.

Eric Well, I figured you were –

Henry A 'good' Republican?

Eric Well . . . yes.

Henry I *am* a good Republican. I gave money to the nominee. As I do every four years.

Jason 1 Why are you a Republican, Henry?

Henry Lots of reasons. I'm a businessman. I believe in low taxes, free markets. Why shouldn't I be a Republican?

Jason 2 Hello, *maricon*, you're gay!

Jason 1 But what about the Republican's age-old hostility to the LGBT community?

Henry Compared to the minutes-old embrace by the Democrats?

Tristan Or the Reagan administration's willful inaction during the epidemic?

Henry I bet you can't guess which US President was the first to make meaningful progress toward attempting to stem the spread of HIV in sub-Saharan Africa?

Jason 2 Bill Clinton.

Henry George W. Bush, your former favorite bogeyman.

Jasper Yes, but PEPFAR was aimed at the straight epidemic, not the gay one –

Eric So, Tucker, when you burn the paintings, is it like a kind of ritual?

Tucker I'm completely naked when I do it. Sometimes I cum afterward.

Tristan You're not actually suggesting that Republicans have done more to fight the spread of HIV than Democrats, are you?

Henry I'll throw a real curveball at you, Tristan. The story of the epidemic is mostly told as a triumph of activism and direct action. But I believe it can just as accurately be told as a triumph of free market principles – and of innovation.

Tristan Please, Henry, do pitch that ball.

Henry When the epidemic began, we knew absolutely nothing about the virus, right? And, within a period of roughly thirteen years, we had identified it, learned its pathology and begun successful drug treatments. You'd have to look at the Manhattan Project to find a faster timeline. And how was it accomplished? It –

Jasper It was accomplished because activists fought for –

Henry Forgive me, Jasper, that was a rhetorical question – it was accomplished because scientists and pharmaceutical companies took the initiative despite intransigent gridlock within the FDA –

Jasper It was the activists who pressured the FDA to relax standards to fast-track drugs.

Henry – which unleashed the drug companies to begin innovating in ways they'd never been allowed to before. The activists, whether they realized it or not, employed libertarian principals in order to free the drug companies from onerous government oversight –

Jasper The drug companies were forced into action by activists.

Henry No, they were *driven* into action by profit motivation, which ultimately led to the introduction of drug cocktails and, a mere twenty years after the start of the epidemic – to Truvada. We went from absolute ignorance to reliable treatment and the prevention of transmission within twenty years! Those drug companies, like all companies, wanted to make a buck. And in doing so, they ended up saving tens of millions of lives.

Jason 1 Yeah, but that's only half the infected population, Henry. And it ignores that fact that if you're a black gay man in America, your chances of contracting HIV in your lifetime are one in two. And the numbers are almost as bad for trans women of color, sex workers, homeless queer youth. Look, I'm a science teacher. I take your point about innovation. But the truth is that the very people who are most in need of access to Truvada can't afford it, thanks to the same pharmaceutical companies you champion, Henry. Come on, let's be honest – when people talk about the epidemic being over, what they really mean is that it's over among middle-class white men.

Henry Jason, my God – one in two?

Jason 1 You won't read about *that* in the *Wall Street Journal*.

Jason 2 You know, I don't think gay people should have to pay taxes.

Henry You don't, huh?

Jason 2 Absolutely not! Why the fuck should I pay taxes to a government that wants to deny me all my rights? Same for women, transfolk, immigrants, and all people of color.

Tristan (*to Jason 2*) We could get a double rebate for that.

Jason 2 Walk into your accounts's office: 'Oh yes, I'll take two oppression exemptions, please.' Actually, we should be able to choose where our tax money goes every year. They could make it look like a Dim Sum menu, you know? And there should be a comments section! 'Dear Mr Government – you may not spend my tax money on war, discrimination or to build any motherfucking walls.'

Henry Jason – I hate to break this to you, but that was spoken like a true libertarian.

Jason 2 I'm vers, Papi.

Henry Ultimately what we're talking about here is a difference in philosophy.

Jasper No, what we're talking about here is a difference in morality.

Eric I think what we're discussing is the divide between the responsibility to community and the responsibility to the self, are we not? I mean, I do think it's possible to effect real change in the world by concentrating on the personal sphere and letting the global sphere take care of itself.

Jasper 'Let the global sphere take care of itself'? Have you been reading Ayn Rand in addition to watching old Westerns?

Eric No, I'm just trying to find a link between what you're saying, Jasper, and what Henry is saying.

Jasper There is no link.

Eric But we have to look for one. You know, when I was a kid, I used to stare at the map of the United States in class. And I always thought that America was shaped like an animal in a way. Maine is the head and Florida is the front legs.

Jason 2 Ooh! What are the back legs?

Eric Well, it didn't really have back legs, baby. I was seven. Anyway, it's always caused me to think of America as a living, breathing organism. America is a body. And you could break down the metaphor all the way to the cellular level if you want. The cells are the American people. And in order to maintain the health of the American body, we have to maintain a healthy relationship with each other.

Henry God, I love how you think. Heal the cells and the body will become healthy. Correct me if I'm wrong, Tristan – but isn't that exactly how HIV is treated?

Tristan Basically, yes. You know, I'm not just a physician, Henry, I've also been living with HIV for eleven years. If America is a body and its citizenry are its cells, then my question would be: what is its immune system? What protects the health of those cells in relationship to each other?

Jasper Our laws.

Jason 2 Our free press.

Jason 1 Our courts.

Eric Our democracy.

Tristan Yes. Our immune system is our democracy. Does everyone remember taking Bio 101 in college?

Tucker My degree was in individualized study, so . . .

Tristan Okay, so you've got your T-cells.

Tucker What are T-cells?

Tristan So T-cells are the first defense against infection.

Jasper It's like on *Game of Thrones,* baby. And the T-cells are the Night's Watch.

Tucker Oh!

Jasper (*to Tristan*) Go on, he's caught up.

Tristan T-cells buzz around the bloodstream, looking for trouble, sounding the alarm at the first sign of infection.

Jasper Calling for Daenerys Targaryen and her dragons!

Tucker Oh yes, I see!

Tristan Now unlike most other viruses, which attach themselves to all different kinds of human cells, HIV attaches itself exclusively to the T-cells – the very cells that are meant to be guarding against such infections. Now with the T-cells compromised, the body's autoimmune system shuts down. So, getting back to Eric's analogy – if America is a body and its citizenry are its cells and its T-cells are its democracy, then what about that man you gave money to? Where would he fit in this analogy? You could say that he is HIV. And, like HIV, he's replicating his genetic material from tweet to tweet, from person to person, institution to institution, across the entire nation. Consequently, America is now falling prey to opportunistic infections its immune system had once at least been able to fight: fear, propaganda, sexism, homophobia, transphobia, white nationalism. And so, like any person with untreated HIV, this nation has developed the *American* Immune Deficiency Syndrome. Maybe we should just call it what it is and diagnose it properly: America has AIDS.

Henry Tristan, you are brilliant! Will you come work for me? I want to pay you to think for a living.

Tristan Oh Henry! You can't afford me.

Eric Okay, I think we've had enough politics for one afternoon. Would anyone like some cake?

Tucker I'd love some, thanks!

Jasper How much money do you make a year, Henry?

Eric Jasper! You do not need to answer that, Henry.

Jasper Why not? For the sake of debate.

Henry I don't mind, for the sake of debate. It's hard to answer too accurately.

Jasper Ballpark it.

Henry Let's say a quarter of a billion dollars a year.

Tucker Wow. That's a lot of money.

Eric There, Jasper: you have your answer. Who wants coffee and cake?

Jasper Do you think it's possible you might care a little more about what happens to powerless people in this country if you weren't a wealthy white, privileged male?

Henry I wasn't born wealthy, Jasper. And certainly not privileged. Although I confess you do have me on white. My father was a car mechanic and my mother was an elementary school teacher. What do your parents do for a living?

Jasper But surely you agree that there's a difference between being born to the white working class in the 1950s and being born into poverty now. Economic inequality is expanding in this country at an exponential rate.

Henry What do you propose I should do about that?

172

Jasper You could start by paying your fair share of taxes. The Constitution starts with 'We the people,' not 'We the people who have good accountants'.

Henry Okay, let's suppose for the sake of argument that I took all my surplus money and gave it to the poor. Let's suppose that every American does – yourself included. Who gets it? Is everyone included in this scheme or only the pure of heart?

Jasper I wouldn't place an ideological litmus test on it.

Henry So you're willing to make sacrifices –

Jasper Absolutely!

Henry – even for a rural white Southern bigot who hates every single one of us in this room but who is just as much in need of economic assistance as the United Colors of Benetton ad you most likely see in your head when you think so romantically of the poor? When you say 'We the people', Jasper, do you really mean that? Or do you mean 'We the people who agree with me'?

Jasper We could start with the people who have lost their homes so you can build your high-rise condos all over the city.

Eric Jasper, come on.

Jasper Or with the homeless people living in the condemned buildings you routinely grab up for pennies on the dollar.

Henry Jasper, it isn't my responsibility as a real estate developer to end homelessness. Nor is it my job as a billionaire to fix income inequality.

Jasper No, it's your responsibility as a human being.

Henry I am responsible to my family, to my employees, my investors. If homelessness, if income inequality is your passion, then it should be your fight. You and I have different philosophies and therefore different priorities. Just because I don't share yours doesn't make me a villain. No one opened any doors for me nor did me any favors.

Jasper Yes, but what you're ignoring is that, while you may have had humble beginnings, you have been on a glide path to success from the day you were born because you're a white male in America and because of that, doors were in fact open to you that have been resolutely sealed to so many other people in this country.

Eric Jasper –

Jasper You don't give a fuck about our community or this nation because for a man like you, being gay is just a speed bump on your journey. You've arrived at your station in life without ever once understanding suffering or the meaning of adversity.

Henry I pray, Jasper, that you never learn the true meaning of adversity. I pray that you never know what it is like to live in fear for your life. I sincerely hope you're forever shielded from misfortune. But you see, my boy, I wasn't. No one saved me. I saved myself. Whether you realize it or not, whether you like it or not, you are the man you are today because men my age paid for your rights with their lives.

Jasper I didn't mean that gay men your age / didn't –

Henry THERE ARE NO GAY MEN MY AGE.
Not nearly enough.

A moment, then:

Gentlemen, it has been an enjoyable if pugnacious afternoon. A pleasure to meet you all.

Eric Henry, please don't go.

Henry I'll be upstairs if you need me. I have some calls to return. Tucker, if you ever want to sell me one of your paintings, I promise I'll never look at it.

He exits. Seething silence, then:

Eric Jasper, I don't even know what to say to you right now.

Jasper You don't know what to say to *me*? Eric, do you see the person you're mixed up with?

Eric That 'person' has a name. He also has a home and you are inside it. You searched his political contributions online and then threw it in his face.

Jason 2 You were pretty nasty about it, Jasper.

Jasper Guys, he is part of the problem.

Eric So then leave his fucking house.

Jasper Fine. Come on, Tucker.

Tucker But there's cake still.

Jasper Look, Eric, I know you've been through a lot this past year or so –

Eric Henry asked me to marry him.

Jasper You're not actually thinking about it, are you?

Eric I don't have to explain myself to you.

Tristan Do you love Henry?

Eric In a way, yes.

Tristan 'In a way'?

Jason 1 Is that enough, Eric?

Jason 2 Are you two fucking?

Eric We haven't yet.

Tristan So what is Henry offering you that you believe you need?

Jasper Besides a billion dollars.

Eric He's offering me happiness and comfort and peace. Why shouldn't I want that?

Jasper Because you'd be throwing away your life, Eric.

Tristan Ignore Jasper.

Jasper No, don't ignore Jasper!

Tristan I'm not saying this because I don't want you to be happy. I'm saying it because I don't want you to be hurt. I'm talking right now about your gorgeous, compassionate heart. Will Henry care for that?

Eric He already does!

Tristan You and Henry are very different people. He's prose and you're poetry.

Jason 1 He's logic and you're passion.

Jasper He's evil and you're not.

Eric I cannot ask you to like Henry, but goddamnit, Jasper, you will respect him. Because he deserves your respect.

Jasper What makes him so deserving of my respect?

Eric The fact that he's won mine.

Jasper Eric, if you marry this man, don't expect me to come to the wedding. And don't expect your job to be waiting for you when you come back from your honeymoon.

Jason 1 Jasper, come on.

Eric You would end our friendship over this?

Jasper I am fighting for our nation's soul. For its very survival. I do not have room in my life for anyone who doesn't agree with that basic truth.

Eric Jasper, this is my life.

Jasper And this is my country.

2. Henry's Study

Henry at his desk. Eric enters.

Eric Henry, I'm so sorry about Jasper.

Henry Don't be. I like all your friends. And they seem to care very much about you.

Eric I've been thinking about your proposal, Henry.

Henry I understand.

Eric I would like to marry you. I would *love* to marry you. If you'll still have me.

Henry I would have waited a lot longer than that. Good. Good!

Eric Should we set a date, or –?

Henry I need to talk to my sons first.

Eric Yes, of course.

Henry Once that's done, I'll call a friend of mine who's a Federal judge and we can get married right away.

Eric Actually, I was hoping we could have the teeny tiniest of parties. We don't even have to call it a wedding. We can call it a 'celebration of marriage'. We can do it at your house in the Hamptons. I promise no more than thirty people.

Henry Yes. Let's have a small, intimate, very expensive 'celebration of marriage'.

Eric Can we have, like, three different cakes?

Henry Let's have a dozen.

Eric Could I have a new suit made?

Henry Of course. One thing: you don't have to ask permission to spend my money.

Eric That's going to take me a little while to get used to.

Henry Once you *do* get used to it, that's when you should definitely start asking permission.

Eric Deal. Holy shit, we're engaged.

Henry Holy shit, we are.

Eric Should I spend the night?

Henry Tonight's not the best for me. And you are far too distracting.

Eric Well . . . before I go . . . I was thinking . . . maybe you should fuck me. Because I really want you to.

Henry Sex isn't really what I'm after.

Eric I understand. It's been a long day. And we've got plenty of time.

Henry Sex has never been that important to me.

Eric Are you attracted to me, Henry?

Henry Yes. Yes, of course.

Eric So . . . will we eventually have sex?

Henry That's not why I want you, Eric.
  I don't care what you do outside of the marriage. All I ask from you is tact and discretion.

Eric How can a man as vital as you not be interested in sex?

Henry I've learned to concentrate on other things. I hope that isn't a deal-breaker for you.

Eric Well, it's . . . certainly a bombshell. Will we share a bed?

Henry If you like.

Eric I'm going to sleep next to you but not get fucked by you?

Henry I wish you'd stop thinking in such absolutes. You should move in as soon as possible.

Eric I just got settled into the Gramercy place.

Henry And now you'll get settled in here. No more moving for a while, how's that sound?

Eric That sounds very nice. Should I bring all my things? My grandmother's furniture?

Henry I have all the furniture we need.

Eric But they're my grandmother's things.

Henry We can store them upstate.

Eric At Walter's house?

Henry It's just sitting there empty.

Eric Walter told me the story of how you found it, and the year you spent living there. He also told me the story of your friend Peter.

Henry Eric, you can't forge a future if you're constantly looking at the past. Do you ever think about Toby?

Eric I try not to.

Henry And why is that?

Eric Because it hurts too much.

Henry There you have it.

Eric That's a different kind of pain and you know it.

Henry But it hurts all the same. You can't help that it hurts. The trick is not minding that it hurts.

Eric *Lawrence of Arabia.*

Henry Gold star.

Eric I just want to make sure I'm not a . . . replacement for Walter. A poor copy of a remarkable original.

Henry When will you ever learn just how special you are? All that matters to me is that you move in as soon as possible. This house gets too quiet without you.

Eric Okay. Thank you, Henry.

    End of Scene Two.

SCENE THREE

Summer, 2017

Toby enters.

Toby Hello boys!

Young Man 7 Oh wow . . .

Young Man 8 Look what the cat dragged in.

Young Man 4 Didn't think we'd see you again.

Young Man 6 Where've you been, motherfucker?

Toby Patiently awaiting my return to the story. So . . . where do we take Toby from here? Remember all those great 'Oh Toby' escapades we used to have?

Young Man 7 Like the time he puked on Meryl Streep?

Young Man 6 Or that time he broke up with Eric?

Young Man 3 And then went directly to Adam's apartment to put the moves on him?

Young Man 2 Or the time he told Eric he was fucking Adam –

Young Man 6 – and then left all his parents' things for him to deal with.

Young Man 5 Eric, that is. Not Adam.

Young Man 8 Right, because Adam isn't speaking to Toby anymore.

Young Man 4 In fact, most people aren't speaking to Toby anymore.

Young Man 1 Toby doesn't really have any friends.

Toby One may as well begin with Toby's phone call to his agent. (*To Young Man 5.*) I've started working on a new play.

Young Man 5 becomes Toby's Agent.

Toby's Agent Fantastic, what's it about?

Toby Oh, it's gonna be terrific! Filled with themes and ideas.

Toby's Agent Yeah?

Toby Characters and plot.

Toby's Agent Okay.

Toby Dialogue and punctuation.

Toby's Agent You don't have any ideas for a new play, do you?

Toby Nope, not a thing. Fuck it. Toby doesn't feel like working right now. His play is going to Broadway.
So . . . one may as well begin with Toby's . . .
One may as well begin with –

Young Man 1 One may as well begin with Toby's parents.

Young Man 1 suddenly produces the box of Toby's parents' things from Part One.

Toby No.

Young Man 1 One may as well begin with Toby's past.

Toby No, we are not doing that, remember? That's not the story we're telling.

Young Man 1 It's a beautiful afternoon, early summer 2017. Toby's walking past the Strand Bookstore when –

1. Strand Bookstore

Young Man 1 rushes on in a mad dash. He crashes into Toby, a few books go flying from Young Man 1's hands.

Toby Hey, asshole! Watch where / you're –

Young Man 1 Sorry.

Toby Adam?

Young Man 1 gathers up his books and rushes off.

Toby Hey, wait!

Young Man 4 The young man flees, leaving one of his books behind.

Young Man 8 It's a notebook –

Young Man 5 – filled with messy handwriting –

Young Man 7 – and every so often –

Young Man 2 – a poem.

Toby (*calling off*) Hey, you forgot your –

Young Man 3 But the young man is gone.

Young Man 4 And all he's left behind is a handful of poems.

Young Man 6 Toby slips the notebook into his pocket and returns home.

Young Man 5 But then, later that afternoon –

2. *Toby's Apartment*

Young Man 1 re-enters as Leo.

Leo Do you remember me?

Toby Yeah, you almost killed me outside of the Strand today.

Leo Sorry.

Toby We also met last Christmas, didn't we?

Leo Yeah.

Toby What's your name?

Leo I'm Leo.

Toby Right. I'm Toby.

Leo I know.

Toby I tried reaching you a few months ago.

Leo You did?

Toby You never texted back.

Leo Oh. I lost my phone.

Toby But you remembered my address.

Leo pulls Toby's card from his pocket.

Leo Actually, you gave me this the night we met. Remember?

Young Man 6 'Toby Darling, Child of Privilege.'

Toby Have you come here for your notebook?

Leo Do you / have it?

Toby You know, when I used to shoplift, I found it was better to waltz on out like I'd paid. They tend not to notice you that way.

He hands the notebook to Leo.

Leo Thank you.

Toby I read a few of your poems.

Leo You did?

Toby I like the one about the guy who leaves the city and walks all night into the countryside. Something hopeful about it. Very Walt Whitman.

Leo Who's Walt Whitman?

Toby Guess we know what your next shoplifting trip's gonna be.

Leo (*re: the notebook*) Thank you.

Toby That's a great view, isn't it?

Leo Yeah.

Toby You can see the whole city.

Leo It . . . shimmers.

Toby Yeah, I guess it does.
   Do you need anything else, Leo? I mean, besides your notebook. Is there something else you need?

Leo Yes.

Toby What?

Leo Kindness?

Young Man 5 But what Leo actually said was –

Leo Could I take a shower?

Toby A shower?

Leo And maybe wash my clothes?

Toby Would you also like to order room service?

Leo Forget it.

Toby No, wait.

Young Man 6 Toby studied Leo's clothes.

Young Man 8 Rank and dirty.

Young Man 5 Hair greasy.

Young Man 3 Leo smelled.

Young Man 4 And Toby answered:

Toby If that's what you need.

Leo Thank you.

Toby Bathroom's through there.

Leo starts undressing.

Where do you live, Leo?

Leo Around.

Toby What does that mean?

Leo Just . . . you know . . .

Toby Do you not know where you live?

He catches Leo retreating into himself.

Oh.

Young Man 5 And Toby instantly feels the burden of Leo's need.

Young Man 8 Toby likes to be wanted but he hates to be needed.

Toby But as he glimpses Leo stepping into the shower, Toby is reminded of himself at that age, arriving in New York without a penny to his name. Watching Leo, Toby sees how easily he could have shared this boy's fate if Eric hadn't rescued him all those years before.

Young Man 2 And so Toby decides to show Leo kindness.

Toby Do you have anywhere to sleep tonight, Leo?

Leo I'll be fine.

Toby You can stay here if you need.

Leo I don't like staying with clients.

Toby I think we've sailed past 'client' at this point, don't you?

Leo I just mean that I usually charge extra for overnight stays.

Toby I'm offering to help you, kid. It's not like I'm asking you to marry me.

Leo That would definitely cost extra.

Toby Do you at least want to stay for dinner?

Leo I don't want to be any trouble.

Toby I was just gonna order some takeout. Are you hungry? Stay for dinner. Chinese okay? Or maybe Mexican.

Leo I like Mexican.

Toby Stay for dinner, Leo. I insist.

Leo Thank you.

Young Man 2 Leo stayed for dinner.

Young Man 5 And then a movie.

Young Man 3 Toby showed him *The Deer Hunter.*

Young Man 7 And then, breaking one of his cardinal rules –

Young Man 3 Leo fell asleep on Toby's sofa.

Young Man 4 Toby and Leo became inseparable that summer.

Young Man 6 Toby folded Leo into his life as if he'd always been there.

Young Man 8 Leo found himself at Toby's with increasing frequency.

Young Man 5 They never spoke of their pasts.

Young Man 2 Nor really of their present lives.

Young Man 7 A fondness and an intimacy grew between them – a kind that Leo had never experienced before with another gay man.

Young Man 8 Toby bought Leo clothes.

Young Man 5 And a new phone.

Young Man 3 Toby took Leo to Film Forum –

Young Man 4 – to the Whitney –

Young Man 7 – and to Storm King.

Toby And then one Sunday afternoon in July, Toby and Leo returned to the Strand Bookstore – this time to purchase books, not steal them.

3. *Strand Bookstore*

Toby Let's start with fiction.

Leo What should we get?

Toby Excellent question.

Okay, Jane Austen. *Pride and Prejudice*, *Sense and Sensibility*, *Emma* and *Persuasion*.

Leo We're getting *all* of these?

Toby Yes!

Young Man 7 Toby had never read any Jane Austen novels –

Young Man 8 – but in most cases, he had seen the movies.

Toby Okay, James Baldwin! Let's do *Giovanni's Room*, *Go Tell it on the Mountain* and *Another Country*.

Young Man 6 Toby had never read James Baldwin, either.

Young Man 2 But the trick Toby had learned, was to bullshit with conviction.

Toby Now the Brontës!

Young Man 3 And so Toby relied on Eric's education –

Young Man 7   – and began selecting for Leo his ex-fiancé's favorite authors.

Toby   Let's get *Wuthering Heights* for Emily, *Jane Eyre* for Charlotte.

Young Man 8 What about Anne?

Toby Fuck Anne. Grab some Calvino.

Leo Have you always been a reader?

Toby Yes, voracious. Okay, Dickens –

Young Man 3 *Great Expectations*! *David Copperfield*! *Oliver Twist*!

Toby Jesus, did he only ever write about orphans?

Leo Toby, there's your book!

Toby Oh yeah.

Leo There's a lot of copies.

Toby Yeah, what the fuck?

Leo What's it about?

Toby Me. My life. Well, a slice of it.

Leo I want to read it.

Young Man 6 And Toby was instantly in a quandary.

Young Man 8 Which Toby Darling did he want Leo to know?

Young Man 3 Toby the person who stood before him?

Young Man 7 Or Toby the creation Leo held in his hand?

Toby You can see the play instead. Okay, what's next?

Young Man 5 We are off to E now.

Young Man 7 *Invisible Man*!

Young Man 5 Now off to F.

Young Man 2 *The Great Gatsby*!

Young Man 8 And then Leo plucked a book off the shelf . . .

Toby Who'd you get?

Leo E. M. Forster?

Toby Oh yeah? Which one?

Leo (*pronouncing it 'Maur-eese'*) *Maurice*?

Toby It's pronounced 'Maurice'.

Toby It's a gay novel Forster wrote back in the teens.

Leo He wrote this when he was a teenager?

Toby No, numbskull. In the 'teens'. Like now, but a hundred years ago. That's actually Eric's favorite book.

Leo Who's Eric?

Toby Grab it. Also *Room With a View*. Oh and *Howards End*.

Leo Toby, I don't really have anywhere to keep all these books.

Toby Oh.
   Well, you can keep them at my place and then take them whenever you want.

Leo Isn't that what a library is for?

Toby It's not enough to read, Leo. You have to own your own books. I'll get a bookshelf just for you. I'll even buy a chair for you to sit in and read. You can come over whenever you want and spend your days reading Forster and Dickens and Waugh.

Leo Oh my.

Toby Forster and Dickens and Waugh.

Leo Oh my.

Toby Forster and Dickens and Waugh.

Leo Oh my!

   His phone dings.

Oh . . . I have to go.

Toby What, right now?

Leo Yeah, I . . . I just have to be somewhere.

Toby But I thought we were hanging out today.

Leo I know, these plans just came up.

Toby But *we* have plans.

Leo I know, but these are . . . 'plans'.

Toby Oh. Well, say no. I thought we could go to the movies / this afternoon.

Leo I can't . . . He's a regular.

Toby How many regulars do you have, exactly?

Leo A few.

Toby I didn't realize you were so popular.

Leo I don't hang out with any of them in bookstores.

Toby Do you still want your books?

Leo Yes. Very much. If you still want to get them for me. Or just one would be fine.

Toby Can I see you later?

Leo I'll text you. I'm sorry. When he calls, I have to – I have to go.

Leo exits. Toby is left alone with all of Leo's books.

Young Man 4 And that was when Toby realized his only friend in the world was a nineteen-year-old sex worker who had better people to see than him.

4. Rehearsal

Young Man 2 Adam McDowell was just weeks away from making one of the most thrilling Broadway debuts in recent memory.

Young Man 8 Adam McDowell was going to be a star.

Adam Adam McDowell had never been more frightened in all his life.

191

Young Man 2 Rehearsals had been tense from day one.

Young Man 6 Okay everyone, five minutes!

All Thank you, five.

Adam approaches Toby.

Adam Hey, Toby?

Toby Yes, Adam?

Adam I have a question about page 74.

Toby It is often to be found after page 73.

Adam It's this new line you wrote. Elan says: '*Et tu Brutus.*' So you're obviously quoting from *Julius Caesar*, right?

Toby Correct.

Adam Okay, so here's the thing. It's actually '*Et tu, Brute*', not 'Brutus'. *Brute* being the vocative case for *Brutus*, which is of course a second declension masculine noun.

Toby What's your point, Adam?

Adam It's just that you make a point of having Elan be this incredibly well-read and precocious seventeen-year-old. Like, kind of a genius.

Toby Yes, Adam. That hasn't changed.

Adam I don't know if that's true. Because if he's getting basic Latin wrong, then it means he's kind of a fraud.

Toby Fraud?

Adam Yeah, and so I was wondering if we could . . . get it right.

A beat, then:

Toby 'Get it right'?

Adam Yeah, Toby. You probably want to get the famous quote right.

Toby I'd like to hear the line as I have written it.

Adam But what you've written makes no sense.

Toby It makes sense to me.

Adam Then why don't *you* play the fucking scene?

Young Man 6 One minute!

Adam If I were anyone else, you wouldn't think twice about granting my request. But because it's me, because you've decided you hate me / after telling me that you love me –

Toby Keep your voice down, Adam. (*After 'love me'.*) Keep your fucking voice down / Adam. I never told you I –

Adam Oh, I'm sorry, am I embarrassing you?

Toby I never said that I loved you.

Adam You attacked me and groped me / and declared your love for me.

Toby I never groped you! I never groped him.

Adam That night in my apartment in Chicago?

Toby You were telling me a story about getting gang fucked by twenty Bel Ami models!

Young Man 6 And we're back!

Adam Shut the fuck up. Toby!

Toby Oh *now* you feel like whispering!

Adam Please, Toby. Don't push me away. / I need your friendship.

Toby (*exploding*) I'm not your fucking mentor, Adam, and I'm not your fucking friend!

He hurls the script down at Adam's feet.

Adam wants to make a change on page 74. Let's give the princess what she wants.

Young Man 6 Okay. everyone, we're picking back up on page 74, with Elan's line, '*Et tu, Brute.*'

5. Toby's Agent

Young Man 5 Toby gets a call from his agent.
(*As Toby's Agent.*) What the fuck is going on in that rehearsal room?

Toby What do you mean?

Toby's Agent I just got a call from your producers. Tom wants you barred from rehearsals.

Toby They can't fire me from my own play.

Toby's Agent Actually, they can. Adam's filing a complaint with Equity.

Toby What?!

Toby's Agent He says he doesn't feel safe with you in the room.

Toby That little fucker. I'll pull the rights.

Toby's Agent And you will never get produced in New York again.

Toby Why aren't you fighting for me?

Toby's Agent I am, but you are making it really difficult. You threw your script at Adam?

Toby Not at his head! How long am I barred from rehearsals?

Toby's Agent I'm sure it will blow over in a few days . . . definitely by tech . . . I'll see if I can get you into previews.

Toby 'Get me in'?! It's my play! This is fucking bullshit! I'll sue them!

Toby's Agent Take a vacation. Go to the beach. And leave Tom and Adam to their work.

Toby Toby hangs up on his agent, blistering with rage. He's about to call Adam –

Young Man 1 – when a text from Eric appears.

Eric Can we talk?

Young Man 1 And Eric almost instantly gets a reply:

Toby Yes.

6. Bar

Eric *and* **Toby** Hey.

Toby You look good.

Eric Thanks. Thanks for seeing me.

Toby Yeah.

Eric Is this weird?

Toby I thought it would be, but it's actually nice to see you again.

Eric Well, good.
   How are rehearsals going?

Toby Great. Tom's a genius, blah blah.

Eric And . . . and Adam?

Toby Adam's fine.

Eric Tell him, tell him I said hello.

Toby You know, you really do look great.

Eric Did you not mean it when you said it just a minute ago?

Toby I just realized how much I meant it.

Eric Well, thank you.
  I still have your boxes, by the way.

Toby My –?

Eric Your parents' things.

Toby You do look really great, Eric.

Eric Listen, Toby, the reason I asked you here today / is that I –

Toby I'm glad you did because I just realized that there's something I need to say to you.

Eric I'm sure there's a lot we have to say to each other.

Toby Yeah, but it's something I just realized.

Eric Great. But if I could maybe go first –

Toby I made a mistake letting you go.

  Silence, then . . .

Eric Oh Toby.

Toby Wow. It's been a long time since I heard you say that.

Eric Toby, listen, I –

Toby I know, I know. We haven't seen each other in months. And the breakup was ugly. But I can't seem to move on from you.

Eric Toby.

Toby I just . . . You're the only person who's ever really known me. And now seeing you again, being with you, it just feels so right. Like I'm coming home.

Eric Toby –

Toby Oh fuck, Eric, I made such a terrible mistake and I want you back.

Eric Toby you don't / understand.

Toby I love you, Eric. And I'm completely lost without you.

Eric Toby, I'm getting married.

The Grand Canyon.

Toby What?

Eric I'm getting married.

Toby To who?

Eric Henry Wilcox.

Silence. Then Toby starts laughing.

Toby That's – you're good – I – wow you really – I totally fell for that.

Eric I'm not joking.

Toby Okay, Eric. You got me once.

Eric Toby, I'm marrying Henry Wilcox.

Toby No, you're not.

Eric Yes, I am.

Toby Stop that.

Eric I'm marrying Henry.

Toby Why do you keep saying that?

Eric Because it's true.

Toby Fuck you.

Eric Excuse me?

Toby I just poured my heart out to you and you go and do this to me? Fuck you, Eric.

Eric This isn't about you, Toby.

Toby Yes it is! We're together for seven years and then seven *months* go by and now you love him and you're marrying this guy?

Eric You left me, remember? For Adam. My life is none of your business anymore.

Toby Please, Eric. I'm falling apart without you.

Eric I have spent the last seven months in more pain than I have ever been in because of you.

Toby I know. I'm sorry.

Eric And I finally find just a fraction of the happiness I felt with you and you do this to me. It is so unfair of you.

Toby Eric, please.

Eric I really had hoped that you'd –
    I even –

He pulls out an envelope from his jacket pocket.

I had even planned to invite you to the wedding. How stupid am I? Henry was right. You're the past. And I need a future that doesn't include you.

Toby You're making the worst mistake of your life.

Eric No, Toby. *You're* the worst mistake of my life.

Toby But I love you, Eric.

Eric I pray that one day you'll be able to say that to someone and actually mean it.

Eric exits. Leaving the wedding invitation behind. Toby picks it up, looking at it.

Toby Toby leaves the bar, returns to his apartment, grabs his computer and his credit card and, without hesitation, rents a cottage in Cherry Grove through the end of the summer.

Young Man 3 The cost is astronomical.

Toby Toby doesn't care about the fucking cost.

Young Man 5 All Toby can think about is his desperate need to escape the city.

Young Man 8 Escape Adam.

Young Man 6 Escape Eric.

Young Man 7 Escape his play.

Young Man 4 Escape himself.

Young Man 3 Toby then texts Leo:

Toby Do you want to come with me to Fire Island for the next six weeks?

Young Man 3 And Toby almost instantly gets a reply:

Leo Yes.

End of Scene Three.

SCENE FOUR

Summer 2017

1. Fire Island

Young Man 2 Leo had never seen the ocean.

Young Man 4 Never walked on a beach or felt the pull of undertow on his feet.

Young Man 6 His fears –

Young Man 5 – his misfortunes –

Young Man 6 – his entire life history momentarily vanished in the face of such immensity.

Young Man 4 For the first time in his life, Leo felt he had sufficient room to breathe.

Young Man 2 He packed an old roll-behind suitcase that rattled along the boardwalk, filled with the books Toby bought him.

Young Man 3 He would wake early each morning and walk along the beach as the sun was rising.

Young Man 4 Eventually planting himself in the sand to read.

Young Man 6 Leo read like an addict, his mind expanding with every book.

Young Man 8 Gabriel García Márquez.

Young Man 2 Toni Morrison.

Young Man 3 Christopher Isherwood.

Young Man 4 Zadie Smith.

Young Man 5 John Steinbeck.

Young Man 3 Virginia Woolf.

Young Man 7 James Baldwin.

Young Man 6 E. M. Forster.

Young Man 4 Leo opened *Howards End* and from the first sentence, his life forever changed.

Leo 'One may as well begin with Helen's letters to her sister.'

Young Man 8 What was it about Forster that spoke to him out of all the other writers he encountered that summer?

Leo While the world Forster wrote about was foreign to Leo, he understood his characters intensely. They hummed with a human truth – Leo felt their vibrations.

Young Man 8 It was when he opened *Maurice* that Leo understood the reason for his bond with Forster.

Leo Like the character of Maurice Hall, Leo had spent his life feeling lonely and unloved –

Young Man 3 – damaged beyond redemption.

Young Man 2 Leo understood the simple yet powerful connection of a gay man in the early twentieth century speaking directly to a young gay man at the start of the twenty-first.

Leo It was as if Forster was reaching a hand out to Leo to say:

Young Man 4 'I have felt as you feel. You are not alone. I will be with you always.'

Toby Jesus! We're on motherfucking Fire Island! The last thing anyone comes here to do is *read*!

Leo By the end of their first week, Toby and Leo had become regular fixtures at dances, at house parties. Their faces were familiar to people they passed every day on the boardwalk and on the beach.

Toby Have you ever done coke?

Leo I've only ever smoked pot.

Toby Today you're getting an upgrade.

A Dealer approaches them.

Toby Gimme an 8-ball. Plus a teen. What else you got?

Dealer Molly.

Toby Yeah. Six pills. No, make it ten.

Dealer Want any K?

Toby Nah, but gimme some G. Six caps. What else you got? I want something I haven't tried.

Dealer Have you ever tried crystal?

Toby I'm not that kind of gay.

Dealer Tina makes sex amazing. You will fuck like you have never fucked before, I promise.

Toby You wanna try it?

Leo I'll do it if you do it.

Toby (*to the Dealer*) Give us all you've got.

Young Man 3 And of course there was sex.

Young Man 5 Sex was everywhere.

Young Man 4 In the heat of the sun –

Young Man 8 – and the shade of the dunes.

Young Man 6 In the music and the dancing –

Young Man 2 – in the pools and hot tubs –

Young Man 8 – and along the twisty pathways of the Meat Rack.

Young Man 7 Fueled by the crystal, Toby and Leo danced and partied and fucked each other constantly.

Leo Neither of them had ever had sex like the kind they had on crystal.

Young Man 7 Toby devoured Leo's body.

Young Man 8 As if Toby was addicted to him.

Leo Over time, Leo learned to give himself over so openly, so unapologetically to Toby's desire. It approached what Leo suspected might be called love-making. Leo was unaccustomed to men showing interest in his body for anything other than their own pleasure. But Toby took his time. Toby knew what turned Leo on. Toby *taught* Leo what turned Leo on. Toby was the first man to properly eat Leo out. So that's what all the fuss was about! Toby would pinpoint Leo's prostate with his finger. The orgasms Toby gave him. The care Toby took with Leo. What other word for it was there than love?

Hey, Toby?

Toby Yes, Leo?

Leo Have you ever been in love?

Toby Yeah, obviously. Haven't you?

Leo I don't know. What does it feel like?

Toby It is the worst feeling in the world.

Leo Really?

Toby It's just awful – feeling so much of something and not being able to numb it.

Come on – let's go dancing.

2. Party in the Pines

Suddenly, we're in a great dance party. Toby and Leo are in the center of it. High as a pair of kites.

Dealer How are you boys feeling?

Toby Fucking amazing.

Dealer Are you two boyfriends?

Leo Oh, we're –

Toby Yes, we are.

Dealer We should hang out. You two are such a hot couple.

Toby You hear that, Leo? He thinks we're a hot couple.

Dealer My roommates are throwing a party tonight. You should come with me.

Toby We like parties, don't we, Leo?

Leo nods.

Dealer You like this kind of party?

Dealer holds up his phone to show Toby a photo.

Toby Oh shit.

Dealer Yeah. There's a full-on fuckfest happening at my place right now. My friends have been wanting a piece of your boyfriend's hot little ass since you got here. Are you into sharing your toys? (*Then, holding up a packet of crystal.*) Because I'm definitely into sharing mine. Come to the party and you can have all you want.

Toby Have you ever done anything like that before?

Leo No.

Toby Neither have I.

Dealer Come and join us, boys.

Toby Let's do it.

Leo I don't really wanna –

Toby Oh no, come on!

Leo Why don't you go without me?

Toby No! I wanna watch all those guys with their hands all over you. Sucking you. Fucking you. It's why we came here, isn't it?

Leo I thought we came here to be with each other.

Toby Come on – let's go.

Young Man 7 And so Leo went to the party, where Toby watched him get fucked by his dealer and his friends.

Toby (*to Dealer*) What else you got?

Young Man 6 More guys show up, each wanting to have a turn with Leo.

Young Man 8 Some grabbing at him so hard that bruises start to form on Leo's wrists.

Leo Toby?

Young Man 7 Toby watches them sucking Leo off –

Young Man 2 – rubbing his body –

Young Man 5 – eating him out –

Young Man 4 – kissing him all over.

Young Man 3 Someone grabs Leo's hair.

Young Man 4 Another holds Leo down.

Young Man 5 As one by one they take their turn with him.

Leo Toby –

Toby God, baby, you look so hot.

Young Man 6 Everyone is touching Leo.

Young Man 7 Thirty hands, fifteen mouths on his body.

Leo Toby?

Toby I always want to feel like I do right now. This moment, this feeling. I want to live in this moment for the rest of my life.

3. A Cottage in Cherry Grove

Leo They get back to their cottage and Leo takes the hottest shower he can stand. He cleans himself and discovers he's bleeding. He can see it going down the drain.

Leo cleans up as best he can and crawls into bed, grateful that the night is over and he can wake in the morning and return to his books. But when it happens again the next weekend. When it happens every weekend . . .

4. *Toby and Leo's Bedroom*

Toby There you are. Why didn't you tell me you were leaving the party?

Leo I got tired.

Toby You just need a pick-me-up. Richie brought back some coke from the city. Take a bump.

Leo No, I'm good.

Toby Go one, take some. It's not that cheap shit we get from that douchebag dealer. This is some serious celebrity coke. Come on – let's go back to the party.

Leo Let's just stay here tonight.

Toby But everyone's waiting.

Leo But I want to be alone with you, Toby.

Toby Is that my book?

Leo Oh.

Toby You're reading *Loved Boy*?

Leo Yeah. Is that okay?

Toby Why are you reading it?

Leo I was just curious about you. How much of it is based on your life? Elan is supposed to be you, right?

Toby I mean, it's a made-up story.

Leo But based on your life, right? How does it work as a play? Is it Elan all by himself or do you meet the other characters?

Toby Who the fuck knows? Tom and Adam have probably changed / the whole thing by now.

Leo Adam?

Toby Yeah, fuckin' Adam. For all I know, he's had Tom turn it into a musical.

Leo Toby, who's Adam?

Toby What?

Leo Who's Adam?

Toby The kid in my play, why?
   Leo, what's the matter?

Leo The night we met you asked if you could call me Adam. And then when we met again in front of the Strand, your first thought was to call me 'Adam'.

Toby Leo . . .

Leo What does Adam look like, Toby?

Toby Leo, listen –

Leo Show me his picture.

Toby I don't have a / picture of him, Leo.

   Leo pulls out his phone.

Leo What's his last name? Adam what?

Toby Leo, just wait a second . . .

   Leo starts to type on his phone.

Leo, please don't look him up.

Leo How much do I look like him, Toby?

Toby A lot, Leo. You look like him a lot, okay?

Leo Adam McDowell. Wow, Toby.

Toby What are you doing?

Leo Going back to the city.

Toby The last ferry left hours ago.

Leo Then I'll sleep on the beach.

Toby Leo please . . .
    Okay, look – yes, I asked you over that night because you look like Adam. I was completely in love and obsessed and I guess I wanted to act out some fantasy or something. But what I didn't expect was to connect to you like I did – that was real, Leo.

Leo Nothing about that night was real, Toby. You paid me to tell you that I loved you.

Toby Look –

Leo Do I mean anything to you at all? Or am I just here for you and your friends to fuck?

Toby Hey, do not put that on me, Leo. You like that just as much as I do.

Leo No, Toby, I hate it. You like it, which is why I do it. And now I find out that the only reason I'm even in your life is because I look like someone that you can't have? At least I now know what I mean to you.

Toby Leo –

Leo So thanks for the vacation, thanks for the books, thanks for all the new clients. Call me whenever you wanna fuck.

Toby Wait, Leo, please don't go.

Leo Why? Why should I stay?

Toby Because I need you.

Leo That's not a good enough reason, Toby.

Toby Well, it's the only one I have! I swear I don't see Adam in your face anymore. I see you, Leo. You're the best thing in my life. You're the only thing in my life. Please don't leave me. Please don't go.

Leo Leo's head says run, but his heart says stay. And for the first time in his life Leo decides to trust.

5. Toby's Opening

Toby's Agent Toby gets a voicemail from his agent. Hey Toby, just checking in. Give me a call.

Toby Delete.

Toby's Agent Listen, Toby, I've been hearing things about your adventures out on Fire Island. We do want people talking about you as the show starts previews, but this is not what we want them saying. Call me back.

Toby Delete.

Toby's Agent Okay, Toby, here's the deal: you have a play about to open on Broadway. Most writers never get to say that. And I think if you miss your opening night, you will regret it for the rest of your life. I'm begging you, Toby: come back to the city.

Toby Toby's play opens, as all important plays do, on a Thursday. Toby skips the red carpet and slips unnoticed backstage. It is a swirl of activity, all in service of delivering his story.

Adam rushes past on his way to the stage.

Adam Hey, Toby. You made it.

Toby Hey, Adam.

Adam Can you believe this night has finally come?

Toby Yeah.

Young Man 6 Mr McDowell to places, please.

Adam It's good to see you, Toby.

Toby Yeah, break a leg, kid.

Adam *Et tu, Brute.*

Toby God, I fucking hate that kid.

Adam walks onto the stage and Toby's play begins.

Adam (*as Elan*) You won't like me at first, but you will over time.

Toby Toby walks inside the theatre and, standing in the back, he momentarily forgets how to breathe. All those years of struggle and here, finally, is the moment he's been working for all his life. Toby watches his play for the first time in over a year. Toby finally sees that he has created something unquestionably good – and unforgivably false. Toby instantly knows he's made a terrible mistake. He shouldn't be here. He should be miles away, hiding in a bunker somewhere. Anywhere, anywhere but here.

Young Man 4 Excuse me, sir. You need to take your seat.

Toby I'm with the production.

Young Man 4 I've never seen you before.

Young Man 2 Is there a problem here?

Young Man 4 This guy won't take his seat.

Young Man 2 Oh shit, that's Toby Darling.

Young Man 4 Who's Toby Darling?

Toby I'm Toby Darling.

Young Man 4 Well, you still have to take your seat.

Leo Toby, where did you go?

Toby I need to get out of here.

Leo But the play just started.

Toby The play is fucking bullshit.

Young Man 3 Shhh . . .

Leo I like it. It's funny.

Toby Eric was right: I'm a total fraud. My entire life has been a lie.

Young Man 3 Shhh!

Leo Toby . . .

Toby No, Leo, it's true. I once told a lie about myself and then I turned that lie into a book and I turned that book into a play all because I wanted people to think I'm someone I'm not. I've pushed away everyone in my life just to get to this moment. And now I'm here, sitting in this theatre, watching my story, and I'm not even in the motherfucker. I wrote a play about myself and I'm not even in it!

Young Man 3 Would you please stop talking?

Toby Fuck you, I wrote this. (*To Leo.*) Come on, let's go.

Leo But the play isn't over.

Toby I don't care, I can't stay here.

Young Man 3 Shhh.

Leo Are you sure?

Toby Yes, I have to get out of here.

Young Man 3 You are ruining this play for me!

Toby Elan's father dies at the end. *Now* I've ruined it for you. (*To Leo.*) Come on. Let's go.

Young Man 2 And with that, Toby and Leo bolted from their seats and ran up the aisle –

Young Man 4 – creating a major disturbance as they went.

Young Man 7 Even Adam noticed from the stage.

Young Man 3 Was that Toby? Running out of the theatre at his own opening night?

Young Man 7 No, it couldn't be.

Young Man 4 Not even Toby Darling would do something that crazy.

Young Man 8 And yet, when he was a no-show at the party, it was all anyone could talk about.

Young Man 5 Until an hour later when the reviews started to pour in. Toby's play was a smash.

End of Scene Four.

SCENE FIVE

Summer 2017

1. Henry's Hamptons Beach House

Young Man 6 On the morning of their wedding, Eric and Henry woke before dawn to watch the sun rise together at Henry's Hamptons beach house. It was a crisp, clear, bright summer day. For the first time in years, Eric Glass was able to glimpse the future. The guests arrived at eleven.

Eric in a new suit. Henry enters.

Henry Last chance to flee.

Eric In these shoes, are you joking?

Henry You do look very handsome.

Eric Do I? I've never owned a suit as nice as this. It's certainly a step up from my bar mitzvah suit. In fact, I think this suit might've cost just as much as my entire bar mitzvah.

Henry But, God knows, not as much as your wedding.

Eric Thank you for this, Henry. It's more than I could have ever hoped for.

Henry If I do only one thing in life, it will be to get you to see what you are worth.

Overcome with emotion, he pulls Eric tightly to him in a deep, tender embrace.

There will be days when you do not feel as tightly held by me as you are right now. But never doubt my gratitude. You've reminded me what it's like to be hopeful, to respond to life with excitement and wonder. You are joy personified, Eric Glass. And I am so grateful you have chosen to spend your life with me.

Young Man 8 And with that, Eric Glass and Henry Wilcox went outside to greet their guests. They exchanged brief vows. There was music and dancing, there was champagne and a dozen different cakes. Neither Eric nor Henry could remember a more perfect day.

Young Man 2 And then.

Young Man 3 A taxi drove up the gravel driveway toward the house.

Young Man 2 A few heads turned in its direction.

Young Man 3 Most did not notice.

Eric But Eric did.

Young Man 4 For out of that taxi climbed Toby Darling. And with him was . . .

Eric Adam?

Young Man 5 As they drew closer, Eric could see that it was not in fact Adam McDowell –

Young Man 7 – but rather a young man who bore an astonishing resemblance to him.

Young Man 6 Neither he nor Toby looked like they'd slept in days.

Toby enters with Leo in tow.

Toby Eric! Eric Glass!

Eric Toby?

Toby Eric! Get in the car. We can all escape together.

Eric Toby, what are you doing?

Toby I'm rescuing you! Eric, you were right: I'm a fraud and a liar. I can see that now. And I'm ready to tell the truth. But you have to tell the truth, too: you don't love Henry and you know you're making a terrible mistake.

Eric You are coked out of your mind.

Toby You don't need to marry Henry. You don't need his house or his money!

Eric Toby, please don't do this.

Leo Toby, maybe this was a bad idea.

Eric Yes, Toby, listen to your friend.

Toby His name is Leo. He's my boyfriend.

Eric I want you both to leave right now.

Toby You invited us!

Eric Not to do this!

The Jasons approach.

Jason 1 } Is everything okay?
Jason 2 } Toby, you made it!

Toby Oh good! Reinforcements! Jason, tell Eric he's making a terrible mistake.

Leo Toby, maybe this isn't such a good idea.

Jason 1 Toby, what do you think you're doing?

Toby I'm saving Eric!

Leo Maybe we should go.

Tristan Toby, you have *got* to go.

Leo Toby, maybe we / should go.

Tristan Toby, get the fuck outta here.

Jason 1 Come on, Toby, why don't you and I take a walk?

Toby Oh, fuck off, Jason.

Jason 1 Toby, I'm serious, man.

Toby Get your hands off me, Jason.

Leo Toby, please, let's just go.

Jason 1 I'm not going to ask you again, Toby.

Toby Oh fuck you, Jason.
    Eric, I want to make things right with you. I want to make up for everything I've ever done wrong.

Eric Including right now? Only you could crash a wedding you were actually invited to.

Toby It isn't a wedding, it's a *celebration of marriage*!

He grandly swings his arms out and accidentally hits Eric in the face.

Eric Toby, Jesus!

Jason 1	That's it, Toby.
	Jason 1 punches Toby in the face.
Toby	Fuck you, Jason! I think you broke my nose. I'll sue you!
Jason 1	Ow! I've never punched someone before. That fucking hurts!
Jason 2	Baby, holy shit! You just punched Toby in the face!
Leo	Toby, Toby, let's go. We shouldn't be here.
Eric	Toby, leave and take your boyfriend with you.
Tristan	Your nose isn't broken, Toby. Now hit the fuckin' road.

Henry storms on.

Henry What the hell is going on? Toby?

Eric They were just leaving, Henry.

Toby No we were not. We were invited!

Henry Toby, get the hell off my property.

Toby I won't let you ruin his life. Eric deserves to be happy.

Eric I *am* happy!

Henry I'm calling the police.

Eric No, let's just get them back into their taxi and . . .

Leo Henry!

Silence. All eyes on Leo. Henry is frozen. He and Leo stare at each other in disbelief.

Henry What are you doing here?

Leo I'm sorry, Henry. I didn't know.

216

Henry What's he doing here?

Eric Toby brought him. Do you know him?

Henry (*to Toby*) You sick piece of shit. What the fuck do you think you're trying to prove?

Toby Me? Fuck you, asshole. How do you know my boyfriend?

Eric Henry . . .?

Henry Get them out of here.

Eric Henry . . .

Henry Now!

He storms off. Eric looks at Toby.

Eric Leave.

Toby Eric –

Eric *Leave me alone!*

Leo Toby, let's go.

Toby Eric, I'm sorry –

Eric I once loved you, Toby, but I am cured of that. Everything you touch you destroy. You are unhappy and unloved because you deserve to be. I now understand why your father killed himself, why your mother drank herself to death. They did it to get as far away from you as possible. They didn't abandon you, Toby, they fled from you like the disease that you are. You wanna start telling the truth? Start telling yourself this truth, Toby: you will spend your life alone and, like your parents, you will die alone. I just hope for this boy's sake it happens sooner rather than later.

Eric runs off. The Lads follow. Toby and Leo are alone.

217

Leo Toby?

Toby Toby wants to reach for Eric. To rewind the last three minutes. He'd do it differently. He'd do it all differently.

Leo Toby, let's go.

Toby He would rewind to that morning, to the day he left Eric, to the moment he first reached out to Adam with desire, to the day his father died. He would rewind until the tape snapped free of its moorings and the story of Toby vanished from existence. But he doesn't reach for Eric and he cannot rewind his story. Toby can only go forward. But he doesn't know how.

End of Act One.

Act Two

Summer 2017–Spring 2018

SCENE ONE

1. Beach on Fire Island

The sound of waves. A full moon shines brightly. Leo sits in the sand, watching the waves.

A figure enters, walking along the shore. He stops, sees Leo. It is Morgan.

Morgan You're out late. Or are you up early?

Leo Both, I guess. You want to join me?

Morgan I probably shouldn't. What would the other characters think? If Toby found out, we'd never hear the end of it.

Leo He won't be up for hours.

Morgan sits down next to Leo. They look out at the ocean, the moon shining in their faces.

Morgan Beautiful night.

Leo I never want to leave here. I love this beach, I love our cottage, I love Toby. I don't know if he loves me?
Were you ever in love?

Morgan I was. More than once. It was not love in the way you might recognize. But it was love to me.

Leo I learned how to fuck when I was fourteen, but no one ever taught me how to love.

Morgan So many of us were never given a healthy example of what it means to be homosexual. Which means, of course, no one ever taught us how to be. How to love, how to accept love. We couldn't find it in our cultures and so we had to find it in each other, didn't we? Clandestinely, fearfully. Sometimes joyfully. Our educations occurred in parks, in public toilets, on these very dunes of Fire Island. Or Hampstead Heath, busier than Oxford Street on some summer nights. It was all dangerous and forbidden and furtive and wonderful. And along the way we hurt each other. Sometimes we caused each other great pain.

Leo Maurice and Alec never hurt each other.

Morgan That's because I ended my story before they could.

Leo I think Toby could hurt me. He has already. And yet . . . all I want is him. I don't think this is going to end well.

Morgan If it's any consolation, no love affair does. Whether by death or dissolution, to fall in love is to make an appointment with heartbreak.

Leo Maybe I should just read about it instead.

Morgan No, you should experience it for yourself, heartbreak and all.

Does the name Edward Carpenter mean anything to you?

Leo No.

Morgan That is regrettable if unsurprising. Edward Carpenter was a Victorian-era poet, philosopher, and one-time Anglican priest. He was the original Radical Faerie. It was rumored he once slept with Walt Whitman, although one does get the impression that a lot of people slept with Walt Whitman. Carpenter lived in the English countryside with his husband George Merrill. Of course, they didn't use that word to describe their relationship but theirs was a true marriage. I visited them in 1912 and you cannot know what it was like at that time to encounter two men living together openly, happily, as a couple. By this time, I was thirty-three, and, while I knew that I was homosexual, I had still never touched another man with desire. The day was getting on and Merrill invited me into the kitchen to help him prepare the dinner. As we talked, ever so deftly, Merrill reached over and touched me, feeling me at the roundest part of my buttock.

Leo He came on to you?

Morgan He made a play. I'd never been touched like that before. It unleashed a creative spring in me unlike any I'd ever felt. Who knew that my creative forces were to be located just north of my buttocks? It was in that instant that I conceived the whole of *Maurice*. I wanted to capture what I saw on that day, to write a simple love story about two ordinary affectionate men. I wanted it to be as revolutionary as Carpenter and Merrill's relationship. And it was imperative that it have a happy ending. The newspapers were filled with too many stories that ended with a young lad dangling from a noose or carted off to prison for his nature. I was determined to change that narrative, at least in fiction. Writing *Maurice* was the most terrifying, and the most exhilarating thing I had ever done. Hiding it from the world was the most shameful. My greatest regret is that I never lived to understand the impact that it had on its readers. If I had even an inkling that you needed to read it as badly as I needed to write it, I might have been braver. But you have shown me that my book was then, as you are now, a link in this chain of gay men teaching one another, loving one another, hurting one another, understanding one another. This inheritance of history, of community, and of self. And from where you sit on this beach today, you have no idea whose lives you will touch, and which ones you will save. But in order to do that, you must love. Even though you know that your heart will be broken by it. The only way to heal heartache is to risk more.

Silence a moment.

Leo Will my story have a happy ending?

Morgan It is only in telling our stories, in living our lives, that we can answer that question. You have already lived quite a lifetime in your nineteen years. Far more than I had when I was your age. I think you are a remarkable person. And I suspect there is the smallest part of you that thinks so too. Perhaps you have more to say than you know.

Silence a moment.

Time for you to continue your story.

Leo Not yet.

Morgan Leo wakes from his dream.

Leo No.

Morgan He is not on Fire Island, he is not with E. M. Forster.

Leo Morgan, please.

Morgan He is back in Toby's apartment, back in Toby's bed.

Leo Leo reaches for Toby –

Morgan But Toby is not there. Leo attempts to recall the events of the night before:

Leo A beautiful wedding.

Morgan But an ugly scene.

Leo Toby's ex, screaming at them.

Morgan And then Leo remembers:

Leo Henry.

Leo calls out for Toby –

Morgan But he gets no answer.

Leo He goes to the living room, hoping to find Toby asleep on the sofa –

Morgan But instead, Leo finds a note in Toby's messy handwriting:
'Leo –
I'm sorry I left without saying goodbye.'

Leo No.

Morgan 'Please take any books you want. Most of them are yours anyway.'

Leo Toby . . .

Morgan 'I wish I were the man you think I am. I can't save you. I can't even save myself. You don't need me, Leo. In fact, you'll be better off without me. I hope you can understand.
'Here's five hundred dollars. It's all I could withdraw at this hour. Take care of yourself.
xo,
Toby.'
And with that, Toby Darling vanished from Leo's life as unexpectedly as he entered it.

End of Scene One.

SCENE TWO

Summer, 2017

1. Henry's Hamptons Beach House

Eric Who is he?
Henry, who is he?

Henry He's no one, nothing.

Eric Didn't seem like nothing to me. How do you know him?

Henry I fucked him.

Eric When?

Henry I can't give you dates.

Eric So more than once? How did you meet him?

Henry I paid for him. He's a fucking prostitute. *You* are the one who invited him into my home.

Eric How long have you been seeing him?
    Henry, answer me!

Henry Two years, off and on.

Eric Why?

Henry Oh, don't be a child, Eric.

Eric No, I mean: why not me? Why don't you want to fuck me?

Henry I'm not having this conversation.

Eric Have you fucked that kid since we've been together?

Henry Yes.

Eric More than once?

Henry Yes.

Eric In our home?

Henry No. He didn't know anything about me until today.

Eric I guess that makes two of us.

Henry I have given you everything I can.

Eric Except yourself. Walter was able to tell me –

Henry I am not Walter! If you married me hoping to find some connection to him, you've made a terrible mistake. One that I will free you of if you want.

Eric What I want is you. All of you. You've asked me to spend my life with you and here I am, in a brand-new suit, willing to give you what you've asked of me but you have given me nothing that actually costs you to give. If I can't have sex with you, then I at least deserve to know why.

Henry Because that would ask more of me than I ever want to give to anyone again. That boy lets me do what I want with him and then he goes away. He does not matter to me. You do. I don't reach out to you for the same thing because you cannot give me what he can.

Eric I've spent these months trying to accept the idea of a sexless marriage but what you're really asking me to accept is a loveless one.

Henry That is not how I see it.

Eric Did you love Walter?

Henry That is none of your business.

Young Walter and Young Henry enter.

Young Walter Yes.

Eric Did you ever need him like I needed Toby?

Young Walter Yes, you did, Henry.

Eric *Were you ever alive, Henry? Have you ever felt anything deeply?*

Young Henry He was so beautiful that day you first saw him. At that rooftop party, in the late afternoon sun.

Henry His hair –

Young Henry – was shining in the light.

Henry His skin –

Young Henry – was luminous and dark from his summer at the beach.

Henry His eyes –

Young Henry – were so –

Henry – honest.

Young Henry Seeing right into you. Wanting you. Drawing you to him. God, how you wanted him.
  I'm Henry.

Young Walter I'm Walter. You're married.

Young Henry No, I'm not.

Young Walter You've got a farmer's tan on your ring finger.

Young Henry God how you wanted him.

Henry He stopped my brain from working. He made the words come out all wrong.

Young Henry You stumbled out of the gate.
  Have you seen *E.T.* yet?

Young Walter Jesus, you've got kids, too?

Henry I think you're beautiful.

Young Henry Round and round you both went. Talking about nothing, though it felt like everything. And then finally, when you couldn't stand to wait any longer:

Henry *and* **Young Henry** Do you want to come back to my place?

Young Walter Will your wife and kids be there?

Henry *and* **Young Henry** They're away for the summer.

Henry Come back to my place.

Young Walter What if I never want to leave?

Young Henry And in that moment, you knew you didn't want him to. And so you said:

Henry Would that be such a bad thing?

Young Henry Finally, you left. Your legs could not move fast enough as you ran the four blocks to your sublet.

Young Walter Racing up the stairs.

Young Henry Five fucking flights.

Young Walter You maneuvered so that I was in front of you.

Young Henry So you could stare at his ass.

Young Walter Finally into the apartment.

Young Henry Both completely naked by the time you hit the bed.

Young Walter God how you fucked me.

Henry God how I wanted him.

Young Henry God how you loved him. How it felt to swallow all the shame, the guilt, the fear.

Young Walter And to listen to those four words escape from your lips –

Young Henry – as you exploded inside him:

Henry I love you, Walter.

Young Walter Finally, after years of fighting against it, after a lifetime of shame –

Henry – to hold you in my arms –

Young Henry – delighting in his body –

Henry – in your smell –

Young Walter – in my skin –

Henry – in your warm breath on my shoulder:

Young Walter I love you, Henry.

Young Henry And to know the peace that comes from finally telling the truth about yourself, about your heart.

Young Walter Then you asked me to stay.

Young Henry Not just that night.

Young Walter But for hundreds, thousands, ten thousand nights after that.

Eric When did you stop loving him, Henry? When did that end?

Young Henry That day at the house.

Henry I'd been in London, working.

Young Henry Hiding. Men were dying there too, but you didn't know their names.

Henry I flew home to surprise you.

Young Walter I ran across the yard to you.

Henry Barefoot.

Young Henry I almost called from the airport but I wanted to see the look on your face as I pulled up.

Young Walter Henry . . .

Henry God, I've missed you.

Young Walter Henry, Peter is here.

Henry Peter?

Young Henry Peter?

Eric Peter West.

Young Henry He's visiting?

Young Walter He's dying.

Henry He came here?

Young Walter I brought him here.

Young Henry To the home you bought to save him, to save yourself.

Young Walter He had nowhere else to go.

Henry What room is he in?

Young Walter Upstairs, in the room across from ours.

Young Henry The room where your kids sleep.

Henry Get him out of there.

Young Henry No, you screamed at him.

Henry *You brought that disease into our home!*

Young Walter Henry, our friend is dying.

Young Henry After all these years, you can still see Walter's face in that moment, contorted with fear and confusion.

Eric *and* **Young Walter** Look at me.

Henry I can't.

Young Walter He is our responsibility.

Henry I'm responsible to you, to my boys, to myself and to no one else.

Eric You got back in the car.

Young Walter Henry!

Eric You drove away.

Young Walter You left me alone.

Eric Without so much as a phone call.

Young Henry And then, months later –

Young Walter I don't want to do this, Henry.

Young Henry Do you want to sell it, then?

Young Walter No. I want that house to be what it has always been to us.

Young Henry If anything were to happen to me –

Young Walter Nothing is going to happen to you.

Young Henry You could sell it, live in it, leave it to whomever you choose.

Eric Henry, if you keep running from this –

Young Walter – from what happened at that house, from what is happening to our friends, to our community –

Eric *and* **Young Walter** – you will never know peace.

Henry *and* **Young Henry** That is my decision.

Young Henry You decided that no house, no community, no nation would ever be strong enough to save you.

Eric You had to save yourself.

Young Henry You had to turn off the part of you that fears. The part that reaches with desire.

Eric The part that loves.

Henry I couldn't touch another man without thinking about death.

Young Henry And so you never touched him again. Your mouth never uttered the words 'I love you' ever again.

Henry Men were dying all around me. Men I knew. Men I loved. My friends. My peers.

Young Henry You decided that if you didn't love him, it wouldn't hurt as badly to lose him –

Henry For thirty-six years I held you at a distance.

For thirty-six years I did not love you the way you needed me to.

For thirty-six years I protected myself from the pain of losing you.

Young Henry And then, after thirty-six years, you lost him anyway. And it hurt just as badly as you feared it would.

Henry And worse because I knew that for thirty-six years, I should have loved you more than I did. I should have held you tighter. I should have loved you more.

Young Henry and Young Walter disappear. Eric and Henry are alone once again.

I can't change the past but I will not stare at it. I choose to close the door on it and leave it where it is. That is my right as someone who was there, as someone who survived. It is my right as someone who cannot close his eyes without seeing the faces of those he lost. If you cannot understand that, if you cannot accept that, if that is not enough for you, then I will release you from this marriage. I've only ever wanted to protect you, Eric. But I can only do that in the way I know how.

A moment, then Eric tentatively reaches to Henry, who takes his hand, holding it.

End of Scene Two.

SCENE THREE

Christmas Eve, 2017

1. David Koch Theater

Young Man 8 Eric Glass was now thirty-five years old.

Young Man 2 Not exactly a young man –

Young Man 7 – but not yet a middle-aged man –

Young Man 3 – he was, quite simply –

Young Man 4 – a man.

Young Man 6 He certainly possessed all the markers of adulthood. In fact, he was able to enumerate them:

Eric One husband.

Young Man 3 One personal trainer.

Young Man 4 One pilates instructor.

Young Man 5 One favorite yoga instructor.

Young Man 8 One primary care physician.

Young Man 7 One dentist.

Young Man 2 One allergist.

Young Man 3 One townhouse in the West Village.

Young Man 4 One beach house in East Hampton.

Young Man 5 One ten-acre farmhouse upstate (empty, used for storage).

Young Man 6 One pied-à-terre in London (Mayfair).

Young Man 7 And one in Paris (the 11th Arrondissement).

Young Man 6 Eric Glass was a fully-fledged, no-fooling, grade-A adult.

Eric And yet, on occasion, Eric would wake in the night to the fear that his life was amounting to nothing, and that his days were accumulating as inconsequentially as autumn snow. Eric wished he had asked Henry more about Walter. He would open drawers and closets whenever Henry was away, as if searching for evidence of his predecessor. But Eric found nothing. Not even a photograph. It was as if the past had been erased as thoroughly from the world as it had been from Henry's mind.

Young Man 3 Christmas Eve arrived, and with it Eric's annual visit with his friends to *The Nutcracker*. Their seats had been upgraded to Prime Orchestra as an early Christmas present from Henry.

Eric Henry, you're going to love this –

Young Man 3 Unfortunately, Henry could not attend because he was preparing for a business trip to Saudi Arabia.

Eric Oh. Well, Eric and Jasper . . .

Young Man 7 Jasper did not join them that year. He had not spoken to Eric in months.

Eric Well, the Jasons arrived –

Young Man 2 The Jasons also begged off, traveling instead to visit family in Pittsburgh for their new son's –

Young Man 8 – first Christmas!

Eric Eric stood by himself in the lobby, waiting for Tristan to arrive.

Young Man 4 The first-act bell rang.

Young Man 3 And Eric stood alone with his two tickets.

Young Man 5 When finally . . .

Tristan enters.

Tristan Hey baby. Sorry I'm late. You know my mom – she likes to yak yak yak. Shall we go in?

Eric Is everything okay?

Tristan Yes, never better.

Eric You're a terrible liar. You know that, right?

Tristan We can talk after the show.

Eric Oh no, is she okay?

Tristan She's fine. Come on, we'll miss the Overture. You love the Overture.

Eric Tristan?

Tristan I told her this morning that I'm moving to Canada in the new year.

Eric What?!

Tristan See? I told you you didn't want to have this conversation right now. Let's go / take our seats.

Eric What are you talking about? Why are you moving to Canada?

Tristan I've taken a job at a clinic in Ontario. They're offering visas and fast-track citizenship to medical professionals willing to work in underserved areas.

Eric You're becoming a Canadian citizen?

Tristan I know, this is huge and they're ringing the bell. We can talk about this after the show.

Eric No, Tristan, please. Why are you doing this?

Tristan I've been thinking about it a while now.

Eric For how long?

Tristan Since the election.

Eric Tristan.

Tristan This whole year has been . . . well . . .
     Eric, this country is destroying itself. And I just can't stick around to watch it happen.

Eric But Tristan, you're an American.

Tristan No, Eric. I'm a gay, HIV-positive black man who lives in America. I don't see how I could possibly have a future here.

Eric Tristan.

Tristan We spent the last eight years pretending we were a better nation than we are. But then Charlottesville happened. And then Puerto Rico. And then Las Vegas. This year has broken my heart. It's stripped away all our fantasies about ourselves and shown us who we really are.

Eric Do you really feel that way?

Tristan Honestly? It feels like America is re-enacting the last thirty minutes of *Titanic* in slow motion – only in this version, they've rammed the boat directly at the iceberg. I ain't drowning for this fucking country. I'm gonna be Kathy Bates, wrapped in my furs, watching the carnage from the safety of my lifeboat.

Eric But Molly Brown wanted to go back and rescue people from the water.

Tristan Yeah, but she didn't. Because she knew she couldn't.

Eric What about the people in this country who don't have that option? What about your patients?

Tristan Eric . . . you married a billionaire that you don't love. You're floating in a gold-plated lifeboat. The rest of us are not as safe as you.

Eric But this country needs people like you, Tristan.

The Nutcracker Overture starts.

Tristan This country doesn't deserve people like me. I don't owe this country a goddamned thing. America isn't worth saving anymore.

But I am.

Tristan exits, leaving Eric alone.

2. Free Clinic

Leo waits in an exam room.

A Clinic Worker enters. He is harried, his mind on a million different things. He sorts through the files in his hands.

Clinic Worker Okay, you are . . . Jeff. No. Danny. No. Leo? Yes. Leo. So what's up, Leo?

Leo I have this cough.

Clinic Worker Is that all you came in wearing?

Leo Um. Yeah?

Clinic Worker It's Christmas Eve. No scarf, no coat?

Clinic Worker starts looking through Leo's file.

We don't have an address for you. Where are you living?

Leo Around.

Clinic Worker Got a working phone?

Leo Not right now.

Leo goes into a coughing fit.

Clinic Worker All right, have a seat.

Clinic Worker inspects Leo's arms.

Leo I don't shoot up.

Clinic Worker Maybe not, but you do have bed bug bites. Okay, let's have a listen. Deep breath. You smoke cigarettes?

Leo Sometimes.

Clinic Worker Pot? Breathe.

Leo Sometimes.

Clinic Worker Anything else?

No answer.

I can't treat you if you don't tell me everything. Crystal?

Leo Sometimes.

Clinic Worker How often?

Leo shrugs.

Once more.

Leo takes a deep breath and falls into a fit of coughing.

You've got bronchitis. If you'd waited any longer it might have turned into pneumonia. I'm putting you on a Z-Pak, plus some steroids and an inhaler. Okay, let's talk about your HIV treatment.

Leo You mean PREP?

Clinic Worker PREP? No. I'm talking about your anti-retroviral treatment.

Leo For what?

Clinic Worker For your HIV.

Leo My – no, I'm not . . .

Clinic Worker That's not what this says.
On your last visit in October . . . your bloodwork

came back positive for HIV antibodies. This is news to you?

Leo That's not possible.

Clinic Worker Why isn't it possible? Have you been having unprotected sex?

Looks like we left a ton of messages. You never called back or came in for a follow-up.

Leo is silent.

You didn't know you were HIV positive?

The phone rings. Clinic Worker answers it.

What?

No, I can't stay late.

I'm driving to my mom's tonight for Christmas. My whole family is expecting me and . . .

Fine, but I'm definitely putting in for overtime.

He hangs up.

Fucking ridiculous.

He turns his attention back to Leo.

We need to take more blood, check your viral load. How many sexual partners have you had in the last six months?

No response from Leo.

Hey, uh . . . (*Looks down at the file.*) Leo. Sexual partners.

Leo I don't know.

Clinic Worker Ballpark it.

Leo Fifty?

Clinic Worker Do you have anyone you can call right now for support?

Phone rings again. Clinic Worker answers.

I'm coming!

Clinic Worker slams the phone down.

Are you sure there's no one you can call?

3. The Streets

Leo Leo left the clinic and wandered the frozen streets. He attempted a mental list of all the men he'd had sex with in the last six months –

Young Man 3 – for money –

Young Man 5 – for shelter –

Young Man 4 – for drugs.

Leo Never for pleasure.

Young Man 7 And of all the men at the parties in The Pines. Which of the nameless strangers had it been?

Leo Leo stood at the end of the Christopher Street pier, the December wind making a mockery of his sweater. He thought of the chain of infection that had been passed down along the years, decades and generations, his particular lineage moving from person to person, until it was eventually passed to him. A bitter inheritance. And yet, despite this chain of humanity, Leo never felt so alone in all his life. Leo looked down at the water, lapping the side of the pier and thought how easily he could disappear into the abyss and never be counted again.

Young Man 4 And then Leo remembered that it was Christmas Eve, one year exactly from the night he first met Toby.

Young Man 7 In the days following Toby's disappearance, Leo had frantically called and texted him until his phone ran out of minutes.

239

Young Man 5 It was possible, Leo thought, that Toby had returned. And, with no way to reach him, Toby had spent the last few months waiting to hear from Leo.

Young Man 6 And so, hoping against hope, Leo made his way to Toby's apartment.

4. Toby's Building

Leo Excuse me.

Doorman 1 No panhandling.

Doorman 2 Get a move on.

Leo I want to see Toby Darling.

Doorman 2 (*to Doorman 1*) Who's Toby Darling?

Doorman 1 (*to Doorman 2*) He lives here. (*To Leo.*) Who are you?

Leo I used to live here, too. With Toby. Do you remember me?

Doorman 1 No.

Leo Is Toby here?

Doorman 1 I can't tell you that.

Leo Can you buzz up to him for me?

Doorman 2 Is he expecting you?

Leo No.

Doorman 2 Then we can't bother him.

Leo I need to see him.

Doorman 1 You can always call him.

Leo I don't have a phone.

Doorman 2 That's not our problem.

Leo Can I use yours?

Doorman 1 ⎫ I don't think so.
Doorman 2 ⎭ Get outta here.

Leo Can I . . . can I at least leave him a message?

Doorman 1 It's a free country.

Leo Leo didn't know what to write.

Young Man 6 'Help me, Toby, I'm in trouble'?

Young Man 5 'Find me, Toby, I'm lost'?

Young Man 6 'Fix me, Toby –'

Leo 'You broke me.'

Eric enters.

Doorman 1 Yes, sir, Merry Christmas.

Doorman 2 How can we help you?

Eric I'm here to see Toby Darling. He's in . . . (*Checking his phone.*) 67C.

Leo looks up.

Doorman 1 Funny. He's also looking for Toby Darling.

Eric and Leo lock eyes. Leo starts to leave.

Eric Oh. You're –
No – please, wait. Leo? Your name is Leo, right? I'm Eric.

Leo I know.

Eric Listen, Leo . . . I came here to see Toby. I haven't heard from him since . . . since the wedding.

Leo That's the last time I saw him, too.

Eric Oh. Do you know where he went?

Leo No. He just . . . disappeared.

Eric (*to the Doormen*) I need you to take me up to Toby's apartment.

Doorman 2 We can't do that.

Eric I'm afraid that something might be wrong. I want to go up to his apartment and see. Can't you let me do that?

Doorman 1 We'd have to call the building manager. It's Christmas Eve, he's got a family.

Eric Or I could call 911 and the police can break down the door. Maybe that'll be faster.

He starts to dial.

Doorman 1 I'll take you up.

Eric Thank you.

Leo I want to come up, too.

Doorman 1 No.

Leo He's my boyfriend.

Doorman 1 Then you should know where he is.

Doorman 2 Of course, we could be convinced to let him up.

Eric takes out his wallet, removes some cash and hands it to Doorman 2.

Eric Now can we please go upstairs?

Young Man 5 They rode up the elevator in silence.

Young Man 6 Eric stole glances at Leo, knowing that the two most important men in his life had both had sex with him.

Young Man 4 Fighting his anger at the young man.

Young Man 7 Fighting his resentment.

Young Man 6 Knowing it was childish of him.

Leo They stepped into the apartment, where Leo had once been so happy.

5. Toby's Apartment

Leo Nothing's been touched since I was here last. Look . . .

He picks up Toby's note.

He left this the night he disappeared.

Eric takes the note, reads it.
Leo moves to a stack of books in the corner, starts looking through them.

Doorman 1 Don't touch those.

Leo These are my books.

Doorman 1 Those are Mr Darling's books.

Eric (*to Doorman 1*) Okay, I think you can go now.

Doorman 1 I can't just leave you here . . . not on Christmas Eve.

Eric takes more money out of his wallet and hands it to Doorman 1.

Lock the door behind you.

He exits. A beat, then:

Eric He said nothing to you about where he was going?

Leo All he left was that note.

He has a coughing fit.

Eric Are you okay?

Leo I'm fine.

Eric Do you need any help or –

Leo I need Toby.

Eric Do you have anywhere to be tonight, Leo? It's Christmas Eve. Do you want to come home with me? For some food, maybe?

Leo I don't think your husband would like that.

A moment, then Eric grabs a duffle bag and raids Toby's dresser, pulling out sweaters and thick woolen socks. He stuffs them into the duffle bag. Eric then grabs a winter coat and hands both it and the duffle bag to Leo.

What are you doing?

Eric Helping you.

Leo I can't take Toby's clothes.

Eric He doesn't need them.

He takes out his wallet, pulls out some cash.

Here . . .

Leo Please stop.

Eric Now I wish I hadn't bribed those guys so much. Take it.

Leo doesn't move.

Leo I don't want your money.

Eric Please let me help you.

Leo Will that make you feel better?

Eric Yes.

Leo takes Eric's money.

Leo Happy?

Eric If these are your books, you should take some of them. (*Starting to investigate them.*) Oh my God, these are all my favorite authors. Wow! You and I have very similar taste in books, Leo.

Leo Toby picked those out for me.

Eric Oh. I see. (*Picking one.*) *Maurice*. I haven't read this in years. God, how I love E. M. Forster. (*Quoting.*) 'How does anything end? One – '

Leo (*also quoting*) 'One should act as if things last.'

   Eric offers Leo the book.

Eric Your book, Leo.

   Leo takes it.

Leo Thank you.

6. Henry and Eric's Townhouse

Young Man 7 Eric returned home, where Henry and his son Charles were preparing for a business trip to Saudi Arabia.

Eric Hello, husband.

Henry I'll be with you in just a minute, Eric.

Charles So the Saudis have just sent yet another agreement.

Henry Oh Christ, what now?

Charles They're now insisting we borrow money from their banks in order to service the fees that they've just added to the lease agreement.

Henry In essence, they want us to borrow money from them in order to pay them the bribe they just demanded. It is, without question, the most breathtaking corruption

I have ever encountered. You have to admire it.

Charles Honestly, Pop – this additional agreement is going to add at least two weeks to the trip.

Henry's Assistant enters, a stack of shirts in his hand.

Henry's Assistant Should I pack two more suits just in case?

Henry Just one. (*To Charles.*) We'll knock that agreement out in three days, Charles.

Eric Henry, I cannot believe you make your assistant work on Christmas Eve.

Henry Oh please, Bob Cratchit would murder Tiny Tim to make what that kid makes in a year.

Eric It's just – surely he didn't go to Harvard Business School to pack your clothes for you.

Henry Harvard Business School is filled with young people who would be happy to pack my clothes for me. (*To his Assistant.*) Isn't that right?

Henry's Assistant I beat out two hundred applicants for this job.

Assistant exits.

Eric Henry, I –

Henry Just a minute, Eric. (*To Charles.*) Charles, I want you to call Deb Randolph at Morgan.

Charles I've already reached out to her.

Henry Good. Tell her we need her to guarantee another half billion in financing, give or take. (*To Eric.*) How was your afternoon?

Eric Oh. Oh, fine.

Henry Did you and Tristan enjoy the ballet?

Eric Oh, well . . .

Charles Paul's on the line. The plane's at Teterboro. We should go.

Henry Yeah, be right there.

Eric Henry, how much money do you have?

Henry I've probably got a couple hundred on me, why?

Eric No, I mean net worth.

Henry That's a complicated answer. How much money, exactly, are you planning to spend while I'm away?

Eric No, I'm not asking for myself.

Henry Who are you asking for, then?

A beat.

Eric Well, when I worked for Jasper, I did something I cared about. And it wasn't just for me, it was . . . for the greater good.

Henry And how does my net worth come to play in all this?

Eric I was thinking I could do something with it. A part of it.

Henry You mean philanthropy?

Eric Yeah, maybe.

Henry I like this for you. What did you have in mind?

Eric Well . . . I follow a guy on Instagram who collects old winter coats and goes around the city giving them to any homeless people he encounters. I could support him.

Henry How?

Eric I could buy him a lot of coats.

Henry That's not philanthropy, that's charity.

Eric I doubt that a homeless person would quibble.

Henry You could also just give a homeless person twenty thousand dollars with which to rent and furnish an apartment.

Eric That sounds even better.

Henry Yes, I'm sure it does. But that's not how you solve homelessness.

Eric It would solve someone's homelessness.

Henry Yes, but you need to think big picture when you're talking philanthropy. You can't get bogged down in minutiae.
   What's brought all this on? Is it because I'm leaving?

Eric No.

   Charles re-enters.

Charles Wheels up in forty minutes, Pop. We should go.

Henry Thank you, Charles.

Eric Listen, Henry – there's / something –

Henry I'm sorry I'll be gone for Christmas. If it were any other place in the world –

Eric I know, Henry –

Henry American businessmen cannot bring their husbands with them to Saudi Arabia.

Eric I understand.

Henry We'll take a trip as soon as I'm back.

   Henry turns to leave, then stops. He turns, approaches Eric and gently kisses him on the lips.

The time will fly by, I promise.

Eric Yes.

Henry exits, leaving Eric alone.

Eric took out his phone and called Toby, instantly getting his voicemail.

Listen, Toby, I know we haven't spoken in a while. I'm genuinely ashamed of the things I said to you at my wedding. You deserved my anger but you did not deserve those words and I am so sorry.

I went to your apartment today, hoping to see you, and when I was there, I saw Leo. Please call me when you can. He needs help, Toby. And I need to know that you're okay. Where are you, Toby?

End of Scene Three.

SCENE FOUR

Spring, 2018

1. The Streets

Leo Leo wakes next to a man he doesn't know in a room he doesn't recognize in a bed he can't remember lying down in.

Young Man 6 Panic seizes him as he searches his body for any signs of disorder.

Young Man 7 He checks for blood.

Leo (None.)

Young Man 2 For cuts.

Leo (A few.)

Young Man 4 For new scratches and for old scars.

Leo (Yeah, both.)

Young Man 6 He then goes about inspecting its internal condition:

Young Man 7 Head fuzzy and pounding.

Leo (Yeah, common.)

Young Man 2 Mouth stale and cottony.

Leo (Okay, normal.)

Young Man 8 Anus slick with lubricant.

Leo (Also normal.)

Young Man 2 Teeth . . . ah, the teeth.

Young Man 6 That's a new development.

Young Man 2 They wobble at the slightest encounter with food –

Young Man 4 – which admittedly is a rare occurrence these days.

Leo He knows they'll eventually fall out.

Young Man 8 If the malnutrition doesn't get them, the meth certainly will.

Young Man 6 Meth.

Young Man 5 Crystal.

Young Man 7 Tina.

Young Man 2 A currency in a world he's descended to, just as his body has become a currency.

Leo Does he sell his body to tweak or does tweaking cause him to sell his body?

Young Man 6 Chicken and egg, really.

Young Man 8 Leo looks down at the man lying next to him.

Young Man 7 Has he told him about his status? That he is HIV positive and detectable?

Leo 'Detectable.' That was the last thing Leo had ever felt in his life. His viral load is the only part of him that registers in the world.

Young Man 5 Leo stands and looks for his clothes, the clothes he's been living in for weeks.

Young Man 3 They reek.

Leo But Leo knows that the real stench comes from him.

Young Man 4 Leo reaches into his jacket pocket and finds his sole possession – his battered paperback copy of *Maurice*.

Leo He can't read it anymore because he can't make sense of the words.

Young Man 2 His malnourished, drug-addled brain is now just a simple processor of binary concepts: day/night.

Young Man 7 Sleep/wake.

Young Man 3 High/not high.

Leo Leo has forgotten how to read.

Young Man 6 Leo glances at the kitchen. The man's wallet rests on the counter, tantalizingly unguarded.

Leo But of all the things he's become . . .

Young Man 8 Whore.

Young Man 7 Addict.

Young Man 3 Transmitter of plague –

Leo Is he also a thief?

Young Man 6 Take the money. You need it.

Leo Leo reaches for the wallet –

Young Man 8 – and his eyes land on a jar of peanut butter. He grabs it, making a beeline for the door –

Young Man 4 – not stopping until it closes behind him, a barrier between him and the money.

Young Man 8 Leo is not a thief.

Young Man 4 Then he looks down at the purloined jar in his hand and revises his assessment:

Leo Leo is not *much* of a thief.

Young Man 4 He steps out into the thin light.

Leo Morning or evening?

Young Man 4 Where is the sun?

Leo Over the Hudson.

Young Man 4 Evening, then. It's pleasant out. Springtime again.

Leo Eight months since Toby abandoned him.

Young Man 4 Leo turns toward the river with his dinner.

Young Man 8 He digs his dirty, sex-smelling fingers into the jar, scooping up a giant mouthful and stuffing it into his gob.

Young Man 4 Pleasure instantly overtakes him.

Young Man 8 He even smiles.

Young Man 5 Even his unhappy childhood cannot erase the pleasures of peanut butter: the gentle touch of his mother's hand on his shoulder, imploring him to eat his sandwich slower.

Young Man 2 His mother, who was the first person to visit her anger and frustrations on the boy.

Young Man 3 For being born.

Young Man 7 For requiring affection.

Young Man 6 For driving away boyfriend after boyfriend by his mere existence.

Young Man 5 And then, later, for attracting their unwanted attention.

Young Man 4 It was never something he initiated or sought.

Young Man 2 The trysts –

Young Man 4 No, the assaults.

Young Man 2 The assaults occurred while his mother worked the dinner shift.

Young Man 4 They were violations, he knew.

Young Man 8 They certainly weren't acts of love.

Leo And yet he had begun to allow himself to believe they were.

Young Man 5 By the time he was fourteen, Leo grew flagrant, audacious. He realized his body was not to be traded away cheaply.

Leo The day his mother discovered Leo and her boyfriend deep into their rut, she kicked out the boyfriend and Leo as well.

Young Man 7 The man gave Leo forty dollars and his first case of chlamydia.

Young Man 3 A week later Leo was in New York City.

Young Man 6 He was seventeen years old.

Leo And now here he is, two years later, eating peanut butter for dinner with no place to go and no one to go to. This is what his life has amounted to.

Young Man 4 He wonders what Forster might say about his current state.

Leo But then Leo remembers that E. M. Forster is dead. And all Leo has of him is one book.

Young Man 5 And, like Leo, that book has started to disintegrate.

Young Man 6 The only difference is that *Maurice* would be remembered and Leo would not.

Leo And, Leo thinks, if that is the case, what's the fucking point of all this suffering? Why go on if no one cares and no one ever will?

Young Man 4 Leo crosses Eighth Avenue –

Leo – and remembers that a hundred blocks north lies the George Washington Bridge –

Young Man 2 – the final resort for so many negations like himself.

Leo Leo turns north and heads toward the bridge, ready to write the end of his story.

Young Man 6 No, he keeps going east.

Young Man 5 Along 45th Street.

Young Man 3 To Toby's theatre.

Leo No.

Young Man 4 Yes. That is what he does.

Leo No, he goes to the fucking bridge.

Young Man 4 Leo goes to Toby's theatre.

Leo No, I can't. Please.

Young Man 3 Leo turns in the direction of Toby's theatre.

Young Man 8 Leo turns in the direction of Toby's theatre.

Young Man 2 Leo turns in the direction of Toby's theatre.

Leo *Please don't make me go on like this!!*

Young Man 8 Leo turns in the direction of Toby's theatre to remember, for a moment, his life before Toby left him.

Young Man 4 The time that Leo was happy.

Leo The time that Leo was loved.
Leo stands in front of Toby's theatre.

Young Man 6 Emblazoned across the doors are photos of Adam.

Young Man 7 The same eyes as Leo's – except Adam's are more hopeful.

Young Man 5 The same lips – except Adam's form more naturally into a smile.

Leo Leo studies Adam's picture and sees how beautiful Adam is. And Leo knows how ugly he is. And he thinks to himself: I'm not the boy you wanted, Toby. I'm the boy you got. And he turns once again towards the bridge.

Young Man 4 And then a voice behind him:

Adam Are you okay? Do you need help?
Hey. What's your name?

Leo I'm Leo.

Adam Hi Leo. I'm Adam.

Leo I know. Your name is Adam McDowell. And everybody loves you.

Adam Do you need help, Leo?

Leo Yeah. I need help.

Adam What do you need? Is there someone I can call for you?

Leo Eric.

Adam Eric? Eric who, Leo?

Leo Eric . . . Glass.

Adam Did you say 'Eric Glass'? How do you know Eric?

Leo Eric was kind to me.

Adam He was kind to me, too. Do you want me to call Eric for you, Leo?

Leo Yes.

Adam Okay, Leo. I'll call him right away.

Leo starts to cry. His knees buckle and he wobbles to the ground. Adam catches him and eases him down.

Leo Please help me. I'm sorry. I'm sorry.

Adam It's okay, Leo. It's okay.

Young Man 3 Two strangers kneeling on the dirty sidewalk, clinging to each other as one of them weeps, creating an obstruction in the path of the people heading toward the theatre to see Adam McDowell perform in Toby's play. A performance that had made Adam a star and, on this night, a performance he would miss.

2. Adam Lucas McDowell

Eric Adam delivered Leo to Eric and Henry's townhouse. Eric fed the young man.

Young Man 8 (Chicken broth and toast.)

Eric Gave him a shower.

Young Man 4 (Expensive soap, French shampoo.)

Eric He gave Leo a clean T-shirt and pajama bottoms.

Young Man 7 (J-Crew shirt, GAP pajamas.)

Eric He put Leo up in a guest room to sleep.

Young Man 6 (Thousand-thread-count bedsheets.)

Young Man 1 Eric and Adam, who had once meant so much to each other, caught up on each other's lives.

Adam I'm sorry to drop all this on you. Especially when we haven't seen each other in so long.

Eric You did the right thing. I'll take care of him.

Adam I think a lot about that summer we spent together. It feels like a lifetime ago. I'm sorry that we lost touch, Eric. It's my fault. I got –

Eric (*with love*) Famous.

Adam Busy. Could I – could we have that friendship again? I didn't realize until just now how much I missed you.

Eric Yes. Yes, of course, Adam. I would love that.

Adam You really are a remarkable man.

Eric No, I'm not remarkable.

Adam No, Eric: you are. How can you not know that?

His phone rings.

Oh shit, it's my producer calling.

Eric Take it.

Young Man 6 And yet, despite their promises to each other, Eric Glass and Adam McDowell would never see each other again after that night.

Young Man 5 Their lives would move in separate directions.

Young Man 7 Eric had come into his life when Adam was most in need of his friendship and he left it once Adam was ready to become the man that he would inevitably be.

Young Man 8 Someone else needed Eric now and Adam had delivered him to his old friend.

Young Man 4 The debt had been repaid.

3. Eric and Henry

Young Man 3 Eric called Henry in Riyadh.

Eric Something's happened that you need to know about.

Henry Are you okay?

Eric I'm fine.

Henry What's this about?

Eric It's about Leo.

Silence from Henry.

Henry? Are you there?

Henry What about him?

Eric He's asleep in our upstairs guest room.

Silence.

Henry?

Henry Why?

Eric He's been sleeping on the streets. He's sick, he's malnourished, and he's deep in the throes of addiction. And he has an untreated HIV infection.

Henry Is he saying I gave it to him?

Eric No, Henry.

Henry Has he come there to blackmail me?

Eric Henry, Leo hasn't come here to blackmail you or to accuse you of anything. He's come here asking for help.

Henry But why has he come to *me*?

Eric He hasn't, Henry, he's come to me.

Henry Where's Toby in all of this?

Eric Disappeared the night of our wedding. Leo hasn't heard from him in over eight months. Henry, he's completely alone in the world.

Henry Well, ah, you should take him to a doctor.

Eric I plan to as soon as he's awake.

Henry Make sure he gets whatever he needs. And, ah, be sure to give him some money to help him get back on his feet.

Eric Henry, Leo needs our help, not just our assistance.

Henry What are you suggesting we do?

Eric I want him to stay with us for a while.

Henry No.

Eric You'll be gone for the next five weeks.

Henry Eric, that is just not possible.

Eric Why isn't it possible?

Henry Because what you're describing is a months-, perhaps years-long undertaking.

Eric Who better than a billionaire to undertake it?

Henry He's not a stray dog you can just bring in off the street.

Eric You make it sound as though he's worse than that.

We can't just fob him off with a few dollars and some kind words, Henry.

Henry And you can't sacrifice yourself to save him.

Eric Why can't I?

Henry Because he isn't our responsibility.

Eric Don't you feel we owe some kind of debt here?

Henry I never gave him drugs. I didn't make him sick.

Eric You and Toby treated him as if he were disposable.

Henry Do not compare me to Toby. Toby's the one who brought him to our house in six different kinds of altered states. He's the one you should be giving this lecture to, not me.

Eric You paid a nineteen-year-old boy to have sex with you. You don't get to take advantage of a desperate young person when it suits you and then turn your back on him when it becomes inconvenient.

Henry Am I responsible for every person I've ever fucked? Am I responsible for every person you've ever met? You cannot save the entire world, Eric.

Eric I'm only trying to save one person.

Henry Which person, Eric? Him or yourself? Get him the fuck out of my house.

4. *The Streets*

Eric Eric stormed out of the townhouse and into the streets of the West Village, raging at Henry's heartlessness. He was furious at Henry for confirming all of Jasper's dire warnings about him. He was furious at Toby, for having once again abandoned a lover – only this time with much more disastrous consequences.

But Eric was also furious with himself. Eric Glass had

spent his life refusing to make waves because he knew that it was in them that the weakest swimmers drowned. When Toby left him, Eric had grabbed the nearest lifeboat and pulled himself to safety, leaving everyone else behind. And on that day in Toby's apartment, it was Eric who had fobbed Leo off with a few dollars and some kind words. Eric had chosen his own comfort over the needs of this frightened young man. And in realizing that, Eric understood that he was no mere witness to Leo's suffering. He was one of its authors.

Eric crossed Seventh Avenue and entered the park in Sheridan Square. Sitting on a bench in his expensive clothes, holding the keys to his 30-million-dollar home, Eric Glass asked himself the simple questions:

'What good am I? To what use has my life been put?'

Eric glanced over at the Stonewall Inn, just across the square from where he sat, where, years before, an unexpected group of people roared their defiance at their powerlessness. Those people did not fear drowning. They built their own lifeboats. They saved themselves. No. They saved each other.

Eric took a breath and looked around him.

What was the responsibility between gay men from one generation to another? What was Eric's role in that continuum? Eric wished he had Walter there with him to ask his advice, to seek his guidance. Walter would have known what to do.

And in that moment, Eric had his answer, as if Walter was still illuminating the path for him even now.

There is a house three hours north of the city that sits unloved and unused. A house that had once been a place where young men went to die. Maybe it could now be a place where they went to thrive.

End of Act Two.

Act Three

Spring 2018

SCENE ONE

1. A Hotel Room in Alabama

Young Man 1 He has a story to tell – it is banging around inside him, aching to come out. But how does he end it? How does he finish his story?

One may as well begin with the night Toby disappeared.

Toby The night Toby disappeared, he took the Acela to Richmond. The end of the line.

He left without a plan. It wasn't until the train arrived in Virginia that he realized where he was going, where his body had reflexively started to travel before his mind caught wind of the scheme.

Young Man 1 He got off the train, took a taxi to the nearest Honda dealership, bought a new Civic off the lot, and drove through the night to his hometown in Alabama.

Toby Hometown. It wasn't his hometown. Manhattan was his hometown. Alabama was where he'd been exiled to as a child.

Young Man 1 He knew where he was headed.

Toby Less so why.

Young Man 1 All he knew was that he had exhausted his options, that his life was unraveling.

Toby He thought of the explorers who first encountered the Grand Canyon. Their first thought must have been 'Oh wow'. Their second: 'Aw fuck. How do I get around that thing?'

Toby knows he's in a similar place and that there's no getting around it.

There's only retreating back up the path, no matter how long you've been traveling it, until you reach the fork in the road where you made your first wrong decision, where you went left when you should have gone right.

Toby has to retrace his steps.

And so here he is – four forty-six in the morning, in the finest hotel room in the state of Alabama.

He was seven when his father died. Toby had in fact been the one who discovered the body slumped in his leather desk chair, his brains splattered across the window behind him, as if yearning for a view of the Hudson River.

Toby's mother didn't come out of her room for days. Her only words to him at the funeral were 'Chin up', which he mistakenly heard as 'Cheer up', for which he resented her for the rest of her life. Not that 'Chin up' was exactly the stuff of wise, motherly direction but at least it had a certain 'Pull yourself up by your bootstraps, we can survive this together' intimation. But 'Cheer up', which is what Toby thought he heard, was unspeakably cruel. He knew in that moment he had lost the wrong parent. He knew, even at the age of seven, that he was well and truly fucked.

Toby and his mother returned to her childhood home in Alabama, a state he had never heard of, let alone visited. Toby's mother lost herself in alcohol the way that a convert loses themselves in religion.

And then Toby Darling, the golden boy, raised in privilege, trained in the violin and in ballet, educated at the finest Manhattan private schools, was deposited in an Alabama public school, where he was anything but the golden boy. Ostracized for his vocabulary, for his sensitivity, for his scandalous interest in learning. No one knew what to do with this sensitive, effeminate, sing-songy, twinkle-toed, wide-eyed, brokenhearted child.

It wasn't long before Toby's new schoolmates smelled the blood in the water.

He was eight when he was first called a 'faggot'.

A moment, then:

He didn't even know its meaning the first time it was hurled against him. He only knew it was not a good thing to be called. He could tell by the way it was flung off the snarling lips of the boy who first uttered it. The hatred in his eyes directed solely at Toby, the only one of his kind at school. The only faggot.

Faggot.

Faggot.

Achingly friendless, Toby would return home to a poverty so crushing he would sometimes go to school for days unwashed. How, when Toby was thirteen, the boy seated next to him complained in front of the entire class that he could not concentrate because he could smell Toby's stinking asshole.

Daily, Toby was sent unprotected into the world to be despised and abused at the hands of people no more worthy than he of God's love yet far more certain of their right to an outsized share of it.

This is the world to which Toby Darling feels compelled to return, now that he is an established, successful, yet no less lost young man. Because he knows he can never truly escape this place – his pain, his humiliation – he's carried with him all his life. Because the words Eric spoke to him at the wedding were the exact words Toby's been telling himself since that day in his father's study. 'Your parents didn't abandon you, they fled from you like the disease that you are. You will spend your life alone and, like your parents, you will die alone.'

And so, four forty-six in the morning, in the finest hotel room in the state of Alabama – Toby faces a choice. Can he accept, can he forgive, does he heal . . . or does he burn himself and everything around him to the ground?

Heal or burn, that is Toby's choice. Heal and grow. Heal and seek truth, dignity and fulfillment. Heal and build a life that is real. Or burn it all – his memories, his past, his anger, his pain, and ultimately himself. Heal or burn. Those are the options before him.

And then Toby finds himself doing something he was never taught to do. Toby prays. Toby prays for guidance, Toby prays for peace. Toby asks God: teach me how to be loved, show me how to forgive those who have harmed me, give me the courage to ask forgiveness of those I have hurt. Forgive my fear, forgive my pain, forgive my doubt. God, please forgive me for being me.

Heal or burn, Toby, heal or burn. You cannot continue on as you have before.

Young Man 1 And so, four forty-six in the morning, in the finest hotel room in the state of Alabama, Toby performs one final, desperate act –

Toby Toby Darling starts to write.

Young Man 1 Toby's new play pours out of him in torrents.

It is born of a creative urge so strong it hurts to keep inside his head.

Toby He labors over it for months, writing and rewriting it furiously in his hotel room in Alabama, barely keeping up with the words as they tumble from his mind.

Young Man 8 His work is fueled by Adderall –

Young Man 6 – and cocaine.

Young Man 7 His sleep is brokered by Ambien –

Young Man 4 – and alcohol.

Toby He calls the new play *Lost Boy*, which is intended as a follow-up to his hit play *Loved Boy*.

Young Man 5 A sequel?

Toby No, a rejection. This play contains all the truths of Toby's life. Stories he should have told Eric. Pain he should have shared with Leo. For the first time in his life, Toby has written honestly. Toby sends it to his agent, gets into his car and drives through the night back to New York.

2. Agent's Office

Toby's Agent So I read your play.

Toby Yeah, and –?

Toby's Agent I had my assistant circle all your typos.

Toby My typos?

Assistant Here's a list of them by page.

Toby Is this a joke? A twenty-page list of my typos?

Assistant You made a lot of typos.

Toby Okay, fine, but what about the play?

Toby's Agent Toby, this script is over four hundred pages! You can't ask an audience to sit through a play that long!

Toby It's a first draft. I can cut it down. But what do you think / of the work?

Toby's Agent It's more than just cutting you need to do. Toby, this play just doesn't make any sense.

Toby That play is the best thing I've ever written.

Toby's Agent No, Toby. *Loved Boy* is the best thing you've ever written.

Toby No, *Loved Boy* was a lie. This is the truth.

Toby's Agent The truth doesn't sell tickets, Toby. I mean: poverty and orphans and unwashed assholes? Nobody wants this depressing shit from you, Toby. It isn't your brand.

Toby Please. You don't understand what this play means to me.

Toby's Agent You vanish for eight months. And now here you are, looking like shit, reeking of alcohol, and you dump this fifty-pound play on my desk and insist that I send it out.

Toby (*Simultaneously*) Look, I know I've been a little –
But I really believe –
I poured my –
I need, I need, I'll need to –
I'll fucking die if I –
Listen to me!! I opened my fucking veins writing this play. You don't know what it cost me to / be that honest.

Toby's Agent I cannot in good conscience send this to anyone, Toby.

Toby Please, please, please, I have nothing left if I – I have to tell the truth.

Toby's Agent Then you need to admit that you've got a drug and alcohol problem.

Toby No, I need you to hear me. I need you to understand me.

Another Agent appears at the door.

Other Agent Hey, Toby, good to see you.

Toby's Agent This is Alex. He's an agent in our sports department.

Other Agent Listen, I know this place in Connecticut. I went there seven years ago. It saved my life. Why don't we go get a cup of coffee and have a talk?

Toby Are you joking?

Toby's Agent We're worried about you, Toby.

Toby I'm not, I'm not going to a fucking rehab.

Toby's Agent We think maybe you should.

Toby I'm not – no – I don't – How dare you?

Toby's Agent We only want what's best for you, Toby.

Other Agent I've been where you are, man.

Toby No you haven't. I'm on top of the fucking world, you're a goddamned sports agent. Go fuck yourself!
Gimme my fucking play.

He grabs the manuscript.

Toby's Agent Toby, please don't do this.

Other Agent The first step is always the hardest, Toby.

Toby's Agent If you don't get help, we cannot continue to represent you.

3. Toby's Apartment

Toby Toby storms into his apartment and quickly drafts an email. Subject line: 'My new play.'
'My former agent refuses to send this out so I fired him and am doing it myself.'
Toby then opens his address book and copies every single person.

Young Man 3 Friends –

Young Man 4 Colleagues –

Young Man 7 Fellow writers –

Young Man 5 Agents –

Young Man 2 Literary managers –

Young Man 6 Artistic directors –

Young Man 8 Studio and network executives –

Young Man 7 Film producers –

Young Man 5 Broadway producers –

Young Man 6 *Times* reporters –

Young Man 2 Former lovers –

Young Man 8 Long lost friends –

Young Man 4 His optometrist –

Young Man 3 Eric –

Young Man 6 Tristan –

Young Man 2 *and* 8 The Jasons –

Young Man 5 Tom Durrell –

Young Man 7 The cast of his play –

Young Man 6 Adam –

All *Everyone!*

Toby A voice inside him tells him to stop and think about this but before he has time to listen, Toby hits send.

Young Man 4 757 e-mails – going, going, going.

Toby And then that voice roars at him: 'Stop! Stop, Toby, for God's sake stop!' And Toby is snapped back to coherence. He reaches for the mouse pad and tries to stop the emails but they keep going.

Young Man 8 Five emails –

Young Man 2 – twenty –

Young Man 7 – fifty emails –

Young Man 6 – one hundred.

Toby Toby tries to disengage the wi-fi, but his trembling fingers won't obey his commands.

Young Man 5 Two hundred –

Young Man 3 – three hundred more emails.

Toby Toby starts to pound on the computer, trying desperately to stop the slow suicide he has just initiated upon his career.

Young Man 4 Five hundred emails sent.

Toby Toby screams. He picks up the computer and smashes it down on the ground.

Young Man 3 Texts and emails begin to pour in almost immediately.

Young Man 8 Toby, it this for real?

Young Man 7 Toby, are you okay?

Young Man 6 Toby, do you realize you sent this to a thousand people?

Young Man 4 Toby, I can't wait to read this.

Young Man 3 Toby, delete me from your contacts.

Young Man 2 Toby, where have you been?

Young Man 5 Toby, you just destroyed your career.

Eric Toby, did you mean to include me in this email? Are you okay? I've been trying to reach you. Call me. I'm going to Walter's house tomorrow. I think you should come and meet me there. I think there's a lot we both need to face.

Toby And then a voice in his head. A voice long dormant, now insisting: 'This is not the man you're meant to be.' And Toby knew what he had to do.

End of Scene One.

Spring 2018

Eric And so Eric traveled once again to Walter's house. Eric tried to engage Leo in conversation but Leo barely uttered a word, watching the farmland of upstate roll past his window. Eric decided to embrace the quiet, taking his time with the drive. Opting for the back roads, over the thruway. He powered off his phone, trusting his memory of the drive he had taken with Henry the year before. They were lost within minutes. But the day was beautiful and Leo smiled as he breathed in the country air through his rattling lungs. Eric could feel a release in Leo's body. They eventually found the house – a place at which Eric had previously spent less than an hour. Eric was almost instantly struck with fear that he was not up to the task of helping this ailing young man, that he had jumped into the water without first measuring its depth. In fact, Eric was terrified. And, strangely, he felt more like himself than he had in years.

1. Walter's House

Eric Here we are. What do you think?

Leo It's nice.

Eric I think so. I think it might even be beautiful. It used to belong to a friend of mine. His name was Walter. Walter loved this house and wanted nothing more than to share it with me, but he never got a chance. I think he would be happy to know that we're here. You and I can explore it together, once you're up for it.

He breathes deeply.

Smell that air. So sweet and clean.

Leo takes a deep breath, then falls into a coughing fit.

Okay. We can try that again later.

Leo That meadow is beautiful.

Eric It is, isn't it? Those wildflowers. You know what? I'll be right back.

Eric runs off toward the meadow. The breeze picks up. Leo closes his eyes and feels it on his face. The sounds of birds and rustling trees and, distantly, a wind chime. He lays down in the grass, the sun on his face. He closes his eyes and rests.

A woman enters. Her name is Margaret. She's in her seventies. She watches Leo a moment. Then:

Margaret Hello.

Leo jumps, startled.

I didn't mean to startle you. You can't be Eric.

Leo No, I'm Leo.

Margaret I'm Margaret. Is Eric with you?

Leo He's in the meadow.

Margaret What do we think of him?

Leo Eric? He's nice.

Margaret Any other adjectives you'd care to use?

Leo He's kind. Gentle. Honest.

Margaret I like those kinds of people.

Leo I don't know many.

Margaret That's because there aren't many.
You picked a beautiful day.

Leo It's peaceful here.

Margaret I think so.
I understand you're unwell.

Leo Eric thinks I'll get better here.

Margaret Do you think you will?

Leo I don't know anymore.

Margaret Come here. There's something I want to show you.

Leo hesitates.

Don't worry. We're not going far.

He then takes her hand, slowly rising. She leads him to the cherry tree.

This tree is over four hundred years old, can you imagine that?
Local histories of this area include stories about this tree. Stories that stretch as far back as the colonial days.

Leo Are those . . . teeth?

Margaret Good eye. Those are pig's teeth. They've been embedded there for centuries.

Leo Why?

Margaret Well, it was once believed that chewing the bark of this tree can cure toothaches and other maladies.

Leo No.

Margaret That's the legend.

Leo Can it?

Margaret No, of course it can't. That's just superstition. The colonists who arrived here from England brought them with them. The superstitions, that is. Not the teeth. Although perhaps both, who knows? What I do find remarkable about that story is that it proves that people have been coming to this place for centuries in search of healing. Like you have.

Eric enters, carrying a bundle of wildflowers in his hands.

Eric Hi. Are you / Margaret?

Margaret Margaret Avery, yes.

Eric Margaret, hello. It's so nice to meet you. I'm Eric, this is / Leo.

Margaret Leo and I have already met. I thought we said eleven.

Eric We did, yes. I'm sorry we're late.

Margaret It's half past noon.

Eric I know. I got distracted by the drive, it's . . . I'm sorry for wasting your time.

Margaret No one wastes my time but me.
  I was telling Leo about this cherry tree.

Eric Yes, the teeth!

He goes to the tree, inspecting it.

Have you been taking care of the house for long?

Margaret I've been living in the area since 1989.

Eric So then you were you here when . . . ?

Margaret I was here when, yes.

Leo When what?

Margaret You haven't told him?

Eric No, not yet.

Leo Told me what?

Margaret But he must know. He must understand.

Leo Understand what?

Margaret Years ago there was a plague. Do you know about it?

Leo Only a little.

Margaret And what little do you know about it?

Leo Many men died.

Margaret That could be said of any plague. What marked this as different?

Eric Many gay men died.

Leo Why did they die?

Margaret I suppose it's because these men's illness required that Americans think about the means by which they contracted it. It required that we look at gay men and accept their nature, accept their affection and their desire for one another as equal to our own. Most people couldn't do that. And so, in our discomfort, we let them die. For years, men came to this house in search of compassion and Walter took them in. He allowed them to leave this world with the kind of dignity they had long been denied while living in it. I know this because one of the men who came here to die was my son. Shall we go inside?

Eric She was reluctant to say more – wanting, it seemed, to unlock the house and continue her day. But Leo kept her in the yard a while longer, pressing her with questions, until eventually, she started to tell them about her son . . .

Margaret He and I were both children when he was born. Only seventeen years apart in age. I was far too young to be given any responsibilities, let alone mother-hood. News of my 'condition' was not met with joy. Had we been Catholics, we might have blamed it on immaculate conception. But we were Southern Baptists and so we blamed it on bourbon.

I named him Michael after my father, hoping it might soften his anger over the pregnancy. You've never seen a girl as frightened as I was the day Michael came into the world. I stared at him as he slept, I slipped my finger into his tiny hands, which he grabbed on to with such strength. That grip, that unwillingness to let go, astonished me. This helpless creature, encountering another human, gripping onto them and holding them tightly, as if fearing that to let go would risk never being held again. It was the first time in my life I understood that I was needed. It was the first time in my life I truly felt love. (*Gesturing toward the house.*) Shall we?

Leo What was Michael like?

Margaret He was kind, gentle, honest. A touch willful, but also a touch fragile. Michael was effeminate as a child. We called it 'sensitive', of course. Others had less compassionate words. I would pray two things about Michael every night: God, please protect him. God, please don't let him be queer.

Leo Were your prayers answered?

Margaret I took matters into my own hands. I bought Michael a set of weights. Michael grew muscles. By the time he was eighteen and announced that he was moving to New York, he stood six foot three and weighed two hundred and twenty pounds of pure, solid muscle. I sent Michael out into the world certain that, however effeminate he might be, at least his imposing physique would keep the queers away.

Well what the hell did I know?

The night before he left, Michael and I stayed up late talking. I kept putting off sleep because I knew that the morning would bring with it his departure. I told him to find a church when he got there and to find himself a nice girl. Get in good with her family, I said. That way he'd be sure to get a decent meal every now and again. And then he told me – and I'll never forget the look of calm, knowing certainty in his eyes as he did – he told me there would be no girls for him, at least not in the way that I meant.

'Mama,' he said, 'I'm homosexual. I'm going to New York to fall in love.'

This was more than I could bear to listen to. 'No,' I told him. 'You're confused. You're afraid. You're still so very young.'

In truth, I was the one who was afraid. Afraid of losing him. Afraid he'd be harmed. Afraid for his soul. I told him he could not be my son and be like that. I told him he would die of disease or violence. I told him he would spend eternity in hell. And do you know what he said to me? 'Well that's better than spending your life in South Carolina.'

I admire the moxy now but that night I wanted to hit him. My only consolation it is that I didn't. But the damage had been done. I was no longer his mother, his protector, his one safe person in the world. In that moment, I made myself a stranger to my son.

If I had known that night that he would only live another seven years . . .

I would have held him in my arms and told him I loved him. I would have placed my hands inside his fist, just like I did when he was a baby. I would have recognized his desperate need for understanding and compassion. I would have shown him kindness.

Leo But you didn't do that?

277

Margaret Nope. I went to bed. I prayed and I cried. I attended to my own needs and I ignored my son's. By the time I woke the next morning, Michael was gone. I didn't see him again until the day he died.

We spoke intermittently over the years. Short, terse conversations over the phone. Christmas, Easter, my birthday. We never talked about his life. I never asked about his feelings or inquired about his heart. Several years went by when I did not speak to Michael at all. Then one day, the telephone rang and a stranger's voice was on the line. He said his name was Walter Poole and that he was a friend of my son's. He was calling to tell me that Michael was sick and that he was taking care of him at his home in upstate New York. He didn't believe Michael had long to live and said that if I wanted to visit, I should come soon.

'Does he have it?' I asked.

'Yes,' he answered.

Walter opened the door for me and I walked inside. I climbed the stairs up to the bedroom where Michael lay. I did not know the man I saw there. I said as much to Walter and he assured me that this was Michael Timothy Avery, my son, aged twenty-five years. Asleep and breathing shallowly and hours away from death. My Michael?

I said to Walter: 'I haven't seen his face in seven years.'

Walter asked me why I came.

'I came to tell him how angry I am at him.'

'Well,' Walter said, 'now's your chance.'

And I stared at my son, hours away from death, and I answered:

'I think he must know by now.'

I walked to his bed. His hair was short and brittle. His face was covered in lesions. He looked older than I did. I looked at his hands. There was fungus growing under his nails. I slipped my hands into his, waiting for Michael to squeeze them as he once had.

I kept my vigil for seven hours. Walter brought me food but I didn't eat it. I couldn't move from Michael's side. The sun was starting to come up. Michael stirred. He opened his eyes. He smiled at me.

'Hi, Mamma,' he said, his voice no more than a croak.

Michael closed his eyes and then squeezed my hand. I sat there for another hour as Michael faded, faded, faded away from me. His grip on my hands weakening until finally he stopped breathing and he slipped between my fingers and died.

Walter had befriended a man whose family owned a funeral home an hour from here. Gay, closeted. Terrified of being outed. And yet every time Walter called, this man would drive over, take each of the men and have them cremated. He'd return with the ashes and Walter would have a ceremony for them here on the property. We buried Michael's alongside the others.

I went home the next day but I couldn't leave this place, not in my mind and not in my heart. I returned the next month and stayed with Walter.

More men came. Men like Michael, who had nowhere to go. Over and over, scenes like that played out in this house, as Walter and I did what we could to comfort these discarded men.

I held their hands as I held Michael's, as if they were my own child. I asked them about their pasts, their dreams that had been thwarted, their lives that had been interrupted and their futures that had been taken from them. Questions I should have spent seven years asking my son. Walter and I buried over two hundred men on this property over the years.

Eric Two hundred?

Margaret There's a list of names somewhere upstairs. Walter knew all of them by heart. I regret I've started to forget them. But only their names. Never their faces.

Those faces have stayed with me all these years, like ghosts. Michael's and so many others. A haunting, if you will. A necessary haunting.

A moment, then:

Shall we go inside? I wasn't given specific instructions. All Henry said was to take care of the things as I saw fit. It took nearly two weeks.

Eric Two weeks? Why so long?

Margaret You had a lot of things delivered.

Eric But the movers were told to leave them in the downstairs rooms.

Margaret Which they did. But then it was left to me to sort it all out.

Eric I don't understand. Sort what all out?

Margaret Your things.

Eric You unpacked my boxes?

Margaret Wasn't I supposed to?

Eric No. We were just storing my things here.

Margaret That was not made explicit.

Eric How much did you unpack?

Margaret All of it.

The house once again appears.

Eric And so, for the second time in his life, Eric entered the house. He stood there dumbfounded as Margaret began to open the shutters and then the windows, filling the room with sunlight and air. There before him was his life in possessions: his books . . . hundreds and hundreds of them. The walls were covered with his artwork and photographs. His old sofa and chairs and lamps and end tables. He had not laid eyes on these things in almost two years.

Margaret For a businessman, Henry can be maddeningly imprecise. 'Make sure it all gets sorted out.' Those were his words. 'Sorted out' does not mean 'stacked in a corner gathering dust'. 'Sorted out' means 'sorted out'. Am I wrong?

Eric No. No, you're not.

Margaret And so . . . out it was sorted.

Eric Everything fits so perfectly.

Margaret This furniture belongs here. Like Walter did. And you.

Eric Me?

Margaret You fit as perfectly here as the books on the shelf.

Leo You own a lot of books.

Margaret Yes he does.

Leo Can I pick something to read?

Eric Yes, of course, Leo. Anything you want.

Margaret I tried to instill some order. They'd been packed haphazardly. Fiction is alphabetized by author. Non-fiction by subject.

Eric I think I'm in love with you.
    Margaret, in all your time caring for this house, have you ever felt the presence of . . . I don't even know how to say this . . .

Margaret You've seen them, haven't you?

    A pause, then . . .

Eric On my first visit. I thought maybe I was imagining things.

Margaret Walter told me about you, in the days before he passed. He said he had found someone he could leave this house to. You remind me of him in a way. I can't tell you how happy I am to know you'll be living here.

Eric Oh, no. I'm not going to be living here. I'm just here for a time. Just while Leo gets back to health.

Margaret You can think that if you want. But this is your home, Eric. You may not know it's yours, but it is. You're living here now and you have been since you stepped onto the property.

Eric Eric and Leo had been at Walter's house for two weeks. Eric attended to Leo's physical, mental and spiritual health, starting him on the medications Eric's doctor prescribed. Margaret would take Leo and Eric to the cemetery on the property and tell them stories of the men who had passed through the house long before them.

Young Man 1 One evening, Margaret brought a photo album as they visited Michael's grave and showed them pictures of him as a child. Leo noticed how happy Michael seemed. He could see in the boy's face a love he had never known as a child. When he told Margaret as much, they wept in each other's arms.

Eric Eric filled the house with wildflowers he had picked from the meadow. Leo grew stronger. The house once again exerting its healing presence. And Eric waited for the moment Henry –

Margaret (or worse, his sons)

Eric – would arrive to throw them out.

Margaret But no one came except Margaret.

Eric And so, when Eric finally did hear a car pull up to the house one twilight, he understood that a reckoning had arrived. He simply had no idea which one.

End of Scene Two.

SCENE THREE

1. Walter's House

Toby enters, looking like utter hell. He holds a few shopping bags in his hands.

Toby I got lost along the way.
  Your directions weren't very . . .
  The house, it's . . . not easy to find.
  I brought groceries. Also, a few bottles of '86 Margaux. And a hundred-year-old bottle of scotch. I can afford shit like that now.

Eric You look awful.

Toby Just . . . livin' the dream, baby.

Eric I read your play. It's a complete mess.

Toby Who are you? Kenneth fuckin' Tynan all of a sudden?

Eric It's also the most courageous thing you've ever written. I should have asked you to tell me more stories about your life when we were together. I can't even imagine what it must've cost you to write. I think I can see what it cost you to write.

Toby I think my career is over.

Eric I think you've got more than just your career to worry about.

Toby I think you may be right.

Eric If it's any consolation, I think my marriage is over.

Toby Well I coulda told you –
Sorry.
I'm sorry.
I need help, Eric.

Eric I can see that.

Toby Will you help me, please?

Silence, then:

Eric Come inside.

Toby makes his way unsteadily inside the house.

Toby Holy shit, it's all our things. Your things. I didn't realize you were living here.
All your books.
Look at that meadow! All those fireflies.

Eric returns. Leo is with him.

Leo Toby?

Toby turns in shocked silence, to see Leo standing there. Then:

Toby Leo. What are you – ?

Leo rushes to him, collapsing into Toby's arms.

Leo Toby.

Toby I thought I'd never see you again.

Leo then pulls away and rushes off.

Toby Leo!

Eric Let him go, Toby.

Toby How did you – where has he –

Leo suddenly re-enters, a glass of water in his hand. He charges at Toby, throws the water in Toby's face and smashes the glass over Toby's head.

Toby falls to the ground. Leo, his hands cut and bloody, advances on him to continue the attack – when Eric grabs Leo and stops him. Leo cries as Eric holds him tightly in his arms, whispering calming, loving words insistently into his ear. Words only Leo can hear. Eric allows Leo to sob as he holds him tightly.

2. Walter's House

Later that night. Toby on the porch, drunk. Eric steps outside.

Toby I should go.

Eric You're in no condition to drive.

The day I met you, I remember thinking, 'This guy is a lot, but this guy is alive.' You shone with life, with promise. And all I wanted was to be next to you for as long as I could.

Toby I hurt you very badly, didn't I?

Eric More than anyone ever has. But I don't think that promise was a lie. I think maybe you looked at the wrong part of yourself when you wrote that play. You looked at the part of you that's damaged. But what about the part of you that's good?

Toby I don't think that part exists anymore.

Eric You know, I still have that box filled with your parents' things. It's up in the attic. I think maybe I've been holding onto it all these years because I hoped that one day you'd be ready to look inside it. Maybe today is that day.

3. Walter's House

Toby Late that night, after both Eric and Leo had fallen asleep, Toby opened his hundred-year-old bottle of scotch and took it with him to the attic. Sitting there on the floor, as if waiting for him, was the box that Eric had been storing for him. Staring at it, Toby realizes he has no idea what's inside.

He steels his nerves and quickly opens the box.

There was no bomb, no snake coiled up waiting to strike. There were just . . . things. Envelopes stuffed with family photos, notebooks filled with his early writing, movie tickets.

A photo of his mother, once so young and beautiful.

And of his father, forever young, robust and handsome.

This is what Toby was so afraid of?

And then . . . Toby finds a photo of himself as a boy, dated two months before his father's death. Toby is standing in his pajamas, staring directly at the camera. So unformed and so trusting. This young boy's only request of the world is that he be loved. Toby stares at the photo, searching for himself in his younger face. He cannot find it. How could this boy have done all the damage that Toby has done? How could this innocent child hurt as many people as Toby has?

And that was the moment Toby understood that he could never heal, because healing was too hard. Toby Darling was only built to destroy. And if he stayed in that house a moment longer, he would continue to hurt – over and over – the only two people he had ever loved. Toby grabbed a pencil and a piece of paper and quickly scrawled across it. He grabbed his keys and fled the house. Toby careened down the empty thruway. Eighty, then ninety, then one hundred miles an hour. Fleeing himself, his history, his shame. And in that last second as his car hurtled toward the concrete wall, Toby wished he had told Eric how much he –

Leo In the morning, Eric goes to the attic and finds Toby's note. Its message encapsulated in two words:

Eric 'I can't.'

Leo Later that morning, a phone call. Eric and Leo are told of an accident on the southbound side of the thruway. A single car, upside down in flames. And inside of it, Toby Darling, who could not heal. Burned alive by the fire that consumed him long before help was called, a lifetime before help arrived.

End of Scene Three.

SCENE FOUR

Spring, 2018

1. Walter's House

Eric They buried Toby's ashes in the small cemetery on Walter's property.

Young Man 8 It was not the funeral Toby had imagined in his darker fantasies.

Young Man 5 There were no celebrities in attendance, no great speeches were given.

Young Man 2 The Jasons drove up from the city.

Young Man 7 Jasper did as well.

Young Man 3 Henry returned from Riyadh.

Young Man 6 Tristan flew in from Toronto.

Young Man 1 Adam sent flowers.

Eric Eric read from Toby's early writing and then, one by one, they bid their friend farewell.

Young Man 6 Eric, as was his nature, made lunch for everyone.

Young Man 1 It was a fine spring day. The house was once again full of people.

2. *Walter's House*

Henry I have to go back to Saudi tonight. It can't be helped.

Eric I understand. Thank you for coming. I know how hard it is for you to be here.

Henry I assume you and . . . I assume you and Leo plan to stay here a little longer.

Eric We do.

Henry I shouldn't be gone more than two weeks.

Eric I'm not coming back to you, Henry.

Henry Eric.

Eric Because I know you'd do everything in your power to make this pain go away.

Henry Yes, of course I would. Why shouldn't I?

Eric Because I don't want it to go away. I have to put it to some use or else all of this will have been pointless.

Henry But there is no point to suffering.

Eric There is if you can learn from it. And I do want to learn from it.

Henry No, you want to torture yourself.

Eric I want to feel things! I want to stop running from the things that frighten me.

Henry Eric, please.

I know that I haven't always . . . I haven't said the things I know you've needed to hear. I've spent the last year trying to find a way to tell you. Maybe I just needed to say the words. I need you, Eric.

I love you.

Eric I love you too, Henry. I do. I was with you because I wanted to be. But I married you because I was afraid not to.

Henry Please don't leave me.

Eric I'm sorry, Henry. But if I don't do this, I'm afraid I'll never do anything again.

I have one thing to ask of you. I know I have no right to, but . . . I wondered if you would be willing to give me Walter's house.

Young Walter and Young Henry enter.

Young Henry And here we are again –

Henry – back where we started.

Eric What do you mean?

Eventually . . .

Henry When Walter was ill, after you had been so kind to him, he wrote your name down on a piece of paper indicating that he wanted you to have his house. I decided at the time . . . I decided it wasn't . . . that it couldn't have been Walter's true desires. So I ignored his wishes, never knowing what you'd come to mean to me in time. And not knowing that Walter had known all along what was best for this house, and what was best for you.

Eric Why did you tell me that?

Henry Because no man should ever have to ask for that which is rightfully his.

3. *Obituaries*

Young Henry And for the second time in as many years, Eric Glass said goodbye to a partner –

Young Walter – and began his life anew.

Young Man 5 Unbeknownst to Eric, Toby had named him the executor of his literary estate.

Young Man 8 He never once saw Toby's play in the two years it ran on Broadway.

Young Man 7 Three years after Toby's death, Eric authorized the publication of his last play. Finally, the world understood who Toby Darling really was.

Young Man 6 Five years after Toby's death and his divorce from Henry, Eric met the man who would become the love of his life.

Young Man 3 They were married at Eric's house upstate, Leo serving as Eric's best man.

Young Man 2 Eric found his path in life by illuminating it for others.

Young Man 4 Without ever planning to, Eric became a teacher, a mentor, and eventually a wise old man to so many who encountered him.

Eric Eric's life was filled with love, with friendship, with family.

Young Man 1 Eric Glass died at the age of ninety-seven at his beloved house in upstate New York. He fell asleep one night while reading in front of the fire and never woke up.

Young Man 6 He was buried next to his husband in the cemetery on his property, and among the countless men who had died there nearly a century before him during the time of the plague.

Young Man 8 Eric's three children, seven grandchildren and fourteen great-grandchildren inherited the house, which they maintain to this day as a cherished family home.

Young Man 4 And what of the young man Leo?

Margaret Leo stayed at Walter's house – now Eric's – for six months after Toby's death.
  While his body was quick to heal, his spirit moved slowly toward recovery.

Young Man 3 He received his GED and enrolled in college.

Young Man 7 Eric paid his tuition from the income he received from Toby's royalties.

Young Man 5 There wasn't a Christmas or a Thanksgiving the two did not spend together for many years.

Young Man 2 When he was forty, Leo met the man who would become his partner for the next twenty-seven years.

Eric Leo rarely felt alone, for he seldom was.

Young Man 1 And, in his later years, when sickness returned or when sadness visited, Leo would think of his life and conjure immense feelings of gratitude for all those he had loved and been loved by.

Eric Leo died in Eric's house, in the room where he always stayed, the room where Walter's friend Peter and Margaret's son Michael had died decades earlier. He was sixty-seven, an age too young by most standards but far older than he ever imagined he'd see. Leo died holding Eric's hand, listening to the sound of the breeze rustling through the curtains.

Margaret The house stood then as it had for centuries and would for centuries more: as a shelter, a refuge, a place of healing; a reminder of the pain, the fragility, and the promise of life.

End of Act Three.

Epilogue

October 9, 2022. Eric's Fortieth Birthday.

1. Eric's House

It is late afternoon on a brilliant autumn day. The cherry tree is aflame in brilliant red and orange leaves. The sun filters through them, casting a golden glow on the house and property.

The yard is festooned with lights and balloons. Off in the distance, the sound of a wonderful party: people talking, laughing, music playing. There's a magical quality in the air.

Leo enters. He approaches the house, having just arrived. He holds a gift bag in his hands. He stares at the house lovingly. Eric enters, sees Leo and rushes to him.

Eric You made it!

Leo Sorry I'm late. I got a late start and then traffic / was –

Eric You're here now, that's all that matters.

Leo Happy birthday!

Eric Thank you.

Leo You're forty!

Eric If we don't say it out loud it isn't true!

Leo I have something for you.

Eric Is it what I think it is?

Leo It is. Although I feel it's a little self-serving as a gift.

Eric No. It's the greatest gift you could ever give me.

Leo hands over the gift bag and Eric pulls out a bound manuscript.

Your first novel. I'm so proud of you.

Eric looks at the cover.

The Inheritance.

Leo Read the dedication.

Eric flips to it and reads:

Eric 'For Eric, who saved me.'
Thank you, Leo.

He then flips to the first page.

Leo Don't read it now!

Eric Just the first page. (*Reading.*) 'One may as well begin with Toby's voicemails to his boyfriend.'

Leo I didn't change his name. I just . . . it didn't feel right to.

Eric I think that's okay. It's the truth.

He closes the manuscript.

Oh Toby . . .
I promised myself I wouldn't cry today and I meant it. I've shed many tears for the dead and I will shed many more before I'm through. But not today.

Henry enters.

Henry Am I interrupting?

Eric Leo was just showing me his book.

Henry Have you finished?

Leo I sent it to my publisher on Friday.

He hands Henry the manuscript.

Henry My goodness. Congratulations. Am I in it?

Leo Yes, but I changed your name.

Henry Good idea.

Leo I called you 'Henry Wilcox,' like in *Howards End*.

Henry I think Walter would have approved.
   Mr Glass?

Eric Yes, Mr Wilcox?

Henry Everyone is waiting for you. We can't have a birthday dinner without the guest of honor.

Eric Right.

   He takes Leo's hand.

I want to show you what I've done with the property.

Leo Did you finally build your dining pavilion?

Eric It's going to be amazing at Thanksgiving.

   Eric and Leo start to go off together. Then –

Aren't you coming, Henry?

Henry I'm actually a little chilly. Do you mind if I borrow a sweater?

Eric Not at all. (*To Leo.*) Come on. We have so many stories to tell each other.

   Eric and Leo run off toward the party.
   Henry then opens the manuscript and begins flipping through until he finds a passage with his name in it. He reads:

Henry 'Henry was caught by the sight of the house. To see it alive once again, the lights inside glowing warmly through the windows. The sound of the voices and music filling the air. The late afternoon light diffused in the brilliant autumn leaves of the grand old cherry tree. How could Walter have known, how could he have seen how things would inevitably be? Henry looked all around him, for the first time he truly saw the beauty of it. Not the property itself, although the property was beautiful. No, what Henry saw was the beauty of his life. A life blessed by this house and Walter and Eric and all his friends both living and long dead. Finally . . .'

As he reads, Leo has quietly re-entered with a sweater. He stands back, listening. Then gently makes his presence known. Henry looks over at him.

Leo 'Finally in that moment, Henry saw it all. The past, the present and the future all at once, all in concert, all around him.'

Eric asked me to bring you this.

Henry hands Leo the book and takes the sweater.

Henry Thank you.

He looks around at the property, puts on the sweater. As he does:
    Walter appears.

Walter Maybe we should plant some bluebells around the perimeter of the house. Or peonies.

Henry is struck by the sight of him. Then:

Henry How about both?

Walter I can't believe we own this. I can't believe all this is ours.

Henry We will be so happy here, I promise.

Walter I believe you, Henry. How could we not be?
    I should probably get dinner started.

Henry No, stay with me. Dinner can wait.

Walter You say that now.

Henry Walter. Forgive me. Please forgive me, Walter. I'm so, I'm so sorry. I wasted so much time.

Walter You have so much left.

Henry What do I do now, Walter? Tell me what to do.

Walter You do what they could not.

He lovingly takes Henry's face in his hands and kisses him deeply.

You live!

The stage floods with golden light. The house glows intensely. Then black.

End of Play.